T0133024

Quality Assurance of Agent-Based and Self-Managed Systems

Quality Assurance of Agent-Based and Self-Managed Systems

Reiner Dumke
Steffen Mencke
Cornelius Wille

CRC Press
Taylor & Francis Group
Boca Raton   London   New York

CRC Press is an imprint of the
Taylor & Francis Group, an **informa** business

CRC Press
Taylor & Francis Group
6000 Broken Sound Parkway NW, Suite 300
Boca Raton, FL 33487-2742

© 2010 by Taylor and Francis Group, LLC
CRC Press is an imprint of Taylor & Francis Group, an Informa business

No claim to original U.S. Government works

Printed in the United States of America on acid-free paper
10 9 8 7 6 5 4 3 2 1

International Standard Book Number: 978-1-4398-1266-2 (Hardback)

Library of Congress Cataloging-in-Publication Data

Dumke, Reiner.
   Quality assurance of agent-based and self-managed systems / Reiner Dumke, Steffen Mencke, Cornelius Wille.
      p. cm.
   Includes bibliographical references and index.
   ISBN 978-1-4398-1266-2 (hardcover : alk. paper)
   1. Intelligent agents (Computer software)--Quality control. 2. Self-adaptive software--Quality control. 3. Software measurement. I. Mencke, Steffen. II. Wille, Cornelius. III. Title.

QA76.76.I58D96 2010
005.1'4--dc22
                                                   2009024575

Visit the Taylor & Francis Web site at
http://www.taylorandfrancis.com

and the CRC Press Web site at
http://www.crcpress.com

Contents

Preface

Self-adapting systems, self-healing applications, corporate global creation, and collaborated robotic teams are current challenges in implementing real intelligent and autonomous software systems that solve, support, or manage worldwide societies and organizations, and community problems of the twenty-first century. Software agent technology is one of the key approaches to implementing such global infrastructures. The importance of the role of quality and quality assurance of agent-based systems and system development grows every day.

Quality assurance has been a main part of software engineering during the last 40 years. This discipline of engineering involves empirical aspects combined with software measurement basics. Software engineering has a large tradition of considering new technologies and paradigms. Figure P.1 shows a simplified paradigm evolution including object-oriented software engineering (OOSE), aspect-oriented programming (AOP), component-based software engineering (CBSE), feature-oriented development (FOD), service-oriented software engineering (SOSE), event-based design (EBD), and agent-oriented software engineering (AOSE).

This book is based on our more than 15 years of experience in software agents' considerations involving agent technology application, agent technology adaptation, and agent system measurement, including performance evaluation and improvements.

This book includes six chapters. The first chapter provides a short overview about the essential basics, aspects, and structures of agent technology in general. The second chapter addresses the main quality aspects in software system development, including different phases of software measurement, evaluation, and exploration.

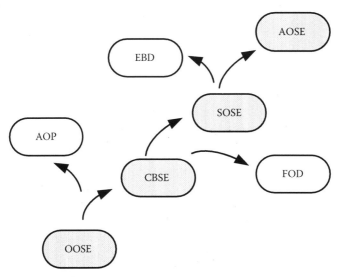

FIGURE P.1 Software engineering paradigms.

The third chapter shows current examples of agent measurement and evaluation with reference to quality aspects and strategies. In the fourth chapter, we discuss the determination of quality properties considering software agent systems and multiagent systems (MASs). The fifth chapter explains different techniques and approaches used to evaluate the development of the MASs. Finally, in Chapter 6, we provide a summary of the quality assurance approaches for agent-based systems and discuss some open problems and future directions.

Reiner Dumke
Steffen Mencke
Cornelius Wille

Magdeburg, Bingen, Germany

Acknowledgments

We wish to express our gratitude to our partners and colleagues who supported us during the last decade in our research in self-managing and agent-based systems. Our thanks go to Professor J. Harrison and Professor J. Munson, University of Idaho, who have helped us in many common works about software agents, security engineering, and dynamic systems measurement. Furthermore, we thank our colleagues N. Brehmer and Dr. A. Lüder for their insight during the European projects "Agent Academy" and "Remote Manufacturing Engineering," where we could learn essential methodologies about quality assurance of dynamic and agent-based distributed systems. The basics of quality measurement were discussed and developed with the help of our research partners Professor A. Abran, Quebec University of Montreal, Canada; Professor S. Stojanov, Plovdiv University, Bulgaria; Professor H. Zuse, Technical University Berlin, Germany; Dr. N. Hanebutte, St. Johns College, New Jersey; Professor O. Ormandjieva, Concordia University, Montreal, Canada; Dr. L. Buglione, Software Engineering Measurement and Quality (SEMQ), Rome, Italy; Dr. M. Daneva, University of Twente, Netherlands; Professor N. Habra, University of Namur, Belgium; Dr. Y. Mitani, IPA/SEC Institute, Tokyo, Japan; and Professor J. Gallego, Alcala University, Madrid, Spain.

We are also grateful to our colleagues at the Fraunhofer Institutes in Magdeburg and Kaiserslautern, Germany, for supporting our research in agent-based system development and evaluation. Furthermore, we express our thanks to our industrial partners Professor A. Schmietendorf, T-Sytems, Berlin, Germany; Dr. M. Lother, Bosch, Stuttgart, Germany; H. Sneed, Anecon, Vienna, Austria; Dr. R. Braungarten, Bosch Rexroth, Loehr, Germany; F. Paulish, Siemens, Munich, Germany; D. Guenther, Volkswagen, Wolfsburg, Germany; S. Frohnhoff, Software Design and Management (sd&m), Frankfurt, Germany; and H. Hegewald, Computer Systems Consulting (CSC), Wiesbaden, Germany, for providing a valuable background and application area for our research and investigations.

Authors

Reiner R. Dumke, Ph.D., is currently working at the Otto-von-Guericke University of Magdeburg, Germany, as a professor, with software engineering as his research field. He is one of the founders of the Software Measurement Laboratory (SML@b) of the computer science department at the University of Magdeburg and coeditor of the *Measurement News Journal.* He is leader of the German Interest Group on software metrics, and he works as a member of the Common Software Measurement International Consortium (COSMIC), Deutsch sprad-rige Anwender gruppe für Software-Metrik und Aufwandschätzung (DASMA), Metrics Associations International Network (MAIN), Institute of Electrical and Electronics Engineers (IEEE), and Association for Computing Machinery (ACM) committees. He received an M.S. in mathematics in 1970 followed in 1980 by a Ph.D., with a dissertation in computer science about the efficiency of database projects. Dr. Dumke is the author and editor of more than 30 books about programming techniques, software metrics, metrics tools, software engineering foundations, component-based software development, and Web engineering.

Steffen Mencke is a Ph.D. candidate and received an M.Sc. in computer science in 2005 from the Otto-von-Guericke University of Magdeburg. As an exceptionally qualified young researcher, he was awarded a Ph.D. scholarship from the German state of Saxony-Anhalt. In 2008, he completed his Ph.D. on the field of proactive content enrichment. Mencke currently works as a research assistant for the Software Engineering Group at the University of Magdeburg. His research interests include agent technology, Semantic Web, and e-Learning, with a special focus on their combination as a basis for consequential advances.

Cornelius Wille, Ph.D., is a professor of software engineering at the University of Applied Sciences Bingen, Germany. He completed his Ph.D. in computer science in 2005, at the Otto-von-Guericke University of Magdeburg after he obtained his diploma in computer science from the same university. Between 2000 and 2004, Dr. Wille was a member of the Software Engineering Group at the University of Magdeburg. At SML@b in Magdeburg, the focus of his work was efficient agent-oriented software development and Web engineering. He is a member of the German Gesellschaft für Informatik (GI) Working Group for Software Measurement and Evaluation and the Association for Computing Machinery (ACM). Dr. Wille is also a member of the International Standardization Organization Subcommittee 7 (ISO SC7) and the German Deutsche Industrienorm (DIN).

1 Software Agent Technology

1.1 INTRODUCTION

To reasonably employ agent technology, it is necessary to understand the underlying software development and engineering concepts. The agent idea goes back to works of Carl Hewitt in the field of artificial intelligence in 1977. He described an object "actor" to be interactive, independent, and executable. Furthermore, it was intended to have an internal state and ability to communicate with other objects (Nwana and Ndumu 1998). Research on software agent technologies originated from distributed artificial intelligence and artificial life. The former main discipline deals with the creation of an organizational system for problem solving, and the latter tries to understand and create models that describe life being able to survive, adapt, and reproduce.

1.2 WHY AGENT-BASED SYSTEMS?

The basic question when applying a technology is its usefulness. When is it possible and beneficial to integrate it? Milgrom et al. (2001) answered this basic question for the agent-oriented paradigm by defining some guidelines validated by case studies (Chainho et al. 2000; Kearney et al. 2000; Caire et al. 2001). Their argumentation starts with a statement that agent-oriented design and implementation will have its greatest scope of applicability in systems with the following characteristics:

- Subsystems and subsystem components forming a system.
- High-level interactions between subsystems and subsystem components in terms of size and complexity.
- Changing interrelationships over time.

Common types of problems that can be solved with agent technology were described in Jennings and Wooldridge (1998) and Ferber (1999). These may include system characteristics like dynamics, openness, complexity, and ubiquitousness, as well as problem qualities like physical distribution of components, data, and knowledge. Agents can be helpful in solving these problems because of their scalability and ability to improve latency (Anghel and Salomie 2003).

The guidelines of Milgrom et al. (2001) result in properties of solutions for complex software problems where the usage of software agent technology is expected to be useful:

1

- *Avoid overkill*: This principle refers to some philosophical background. It is mainly concerned with the adjustment of requirements and solutions. Not everything that is possible to design with agents should be implemented with them. Otherwise, it is a waste of time and effort. "Always attempt to develop the simplest solution possible to any given problem" (Milgrom et al. 2001, p. 102).

- *Need for distributed control*: Decentralized management of distributed systems can be appropriate due to platform, responsibility, privacy, and physical constraints. For the first case, this may emerge due to the intended integration of several applications running on incompatible platforms. Agents can be used to wrap existing functionality and enable their interrelation. Responsibility may cause effects that can be modeled explicitly by agent technology, because complex software systems might work for different owners with different goals. Negotiation algorithms can offer a fair compromise at run-time. Privacy can be achieved by secure agents; privacy policies can simply be implemented. Physical constraints may require agent characteristics, too. A famous example is the complex robot control system for extraterrestrial deployment on missions to Mars.

- *Need for complex communications*: Many approaches exist to realize distributed systems (for example, n-tier architectures, Common Object Request Broker Architecture [CORBA], Enterprise Java Beans [EJB]). Their interaction style is mostly based on several assumptions so the sender knows the intended receiver as well as the appropriate method or procedure to receive the message in addition to the message type to be sent. Agents are useful in situations with a more complex and flexible needed interaction. By limiting the set of message types and extending the included semantic, it was possible to define communication patterns that are directly reusable.

- *Need to concurrently achieve multiple, possibly conflicting goals*: Sometimes system behavior and the corresponding interaction schemes are too complex to be completely modeled at design time. Agent technology solves this problem by defining *how to decide* what to do instead of mapping inputs to outputs by defining *what to do*. Using this approach, a more flexible implementation becomes possible by adapting the behavior of the corresponding agents.

- *Need for autonomous behavior*: This need arises in the case of an absence of explicit requests for action. Software is more flexible if it is able to perform certain actions in a goal-directed manner without continuous human supervision.

- *Need for high flexibility and adaptiveness*: Agent technology's advantage of intrinsic modularity and the possible cognitive capabilities lead to very effective and learning software systems. Agents can be added and removed at run-time, thereby lowering costs because of easy system expansion and modification.

- *Need for interoperability*: Sometimes systems are intended to interact with other software whose specification is unknown during its own design. Using agents is a possible solution, because they can provide services beyond their own capability due to their relations in a multiagent system.

- *Nontechnical guidelines*: Technical aspects are not the only ones that need to be considered. Analysis and weighting of management issues are necessary, too (O'Malley and DeLoach 2002). That includes the cost of acquiring and adopting the methodology for use in an organization, the existence and cost of support tools, the availability of reusable components, the effects on existing organizational business practices, the compliance with formal or de facto standards, as well as the support for the tracing of changes during the software life cycle.

There is almost never an advantage without any trade-off. The nature of the agent paradigm may lead to several problems (e.g., Jennings and Wooldridge 1998; Markham et al. 2003):

- No overall system controller that keeps global constraints and avoids live-locks and deadlocks.
- No global perspective to the whole system or to the complete knowledge.
- Trust and delegation of agents seeking guidance during the time that work autonomously on their behalf.
- Ethical and privacy issues.
- Sometimes bad reputation and lack of trust (viruses are sometimes called agents).

The presented guidelines can be applied in several domains where agents can usefully be applied. One of them might be software measurement. Therefore, the rest of this chapter deals with chosen technical aspects of agent technology for this purpose.

1.3 BASIC DEFINITIONS

No single definition for *agents* exists, but there has been a lot of discussion (e.g., Castelfranchi 1995; Franklin and Graesser 1997; Wooldridge 1997; Wooldridge and Jennings 1995). Almost every author seems to propose his or her own needs and ideas, which leads to a variety of definitions depending on the targeted problem area. The expressed spectrum determines reasonable application areas, such as, for example, user interfaces, telecommunications, network management, electronic commerce, and information gathering (Sánchez 1997). Russel and Norvig described this multiplicity aspect in this way (Russel and Norvig 1995, p. 106): "The notion of an agent is meant to be a tool . . . , not an absolute characterization that divides the world into agents and non-agents." Nevertheless, there are existing definitions.

The Foundation for Intelligent Physical Agents (FIPA) provides a set of specifications representing a collection of standards that are intended to promote the interoperation of heterogeneous agents and the services that they can represent. Their definition promotes an agent as a computational process that implements the autonomous, communicating functionality of an application (FIPA00023 2002).

Another classic definition by Wooldridge and Jennings is based on technology features (Wooldridge and Jennings 1995a). The Wooldridge-Jennings-Agent is a software-based computer system with certain properties, such as autonomy, social ability, reactivity, and proactiveness.

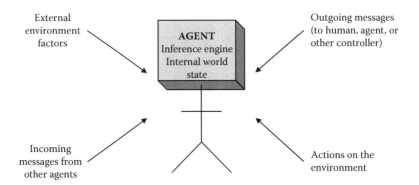

FIGURE 1.1   Agents and their interaction with the environment. (Adapted Hayzelden, A. L. G. and J. Bigham. 1999. *Knowledge Engineering Review* 14: 341–375. With permission.)

The next aspect of agent technology evolves from the following definition. Maes (1994) clearly states that there is an environment needed for any autonomous action. Their autonomous agents are computational systems that inhabit some complex dynamic environment, sense and act autonomously in this environment, and by doing so realize a set of goals or tasks for which they are designed. Franklin and Graesser (1997) use a similar definition. Agents and their environmental context are shown in Figure 1.1.

Other definitions identify agents as "Human Surrogates" that operate autonomously as "Intelligent Assistants" to support human beings, or as an architectural pattern for software development (Jafari 2002; Smolle and Sure 2002). Furthermore, viruses or virus scanning programs are often seen as agents (Markham et al. 2003).

A definition that attempts to define an almost "complete" property set for agent characterization is given in Ferber (1999). They define an agent as a physical or virtual entity that:

- Is capable of acting in an environment.
- Can communicate directly with other agents.
- Is driven by a set of tendencies (in the form of individual objectives or of a satisfaction/survival function that it tries to optimize).
- Possesses resources of its own.
- Is capable of perceiving its environment (but to a limited extent).
- Has only a partial representation of this environment (and perhaps none at all).
- Possesses skills and can offer services.
- May be able to reproduce itself.
- Displays behavior that tends toward satisfying its objectives, taking account of the resources and skills available to it, and depending upon its perception, representations, and the communications it receives.

1.4 AGENT PROPERTIES

Almost all agent definitions have one aspect in common. They are based on certain properties. Every theoretician or developer proposes individual beliefs about potential benefits of his or her system or what is necessary to describe it. That explains the abundance of existing definitions (Kernchen 2004).

Literature differentiates between required and optional properties. The most referenced required properties include:

- *Autonomy*: The most important property is autonomy. It is common to almost all agent definitions. Agents act autonomously when they perform their actions without direct interventions from humans or other agents. They should have control over their actions and their internal state. They significantly differ from "normal" objects in the sense of software engineering in having a behavior. Agents have control over the execution of their methods (Franklin and Graesser 1997; Jennings and Wooldridge 1998).
- *Social Ability*: This ability refers to the interaction potential of this technology. Agents need relations to other agents or humans to perform their actions or to help them perform their tasks (Franklin and Graesser 1997; Jennings and Woldridge 1998). They are communicative for coordination and for exchange and validation of knowledge.
- *Reactivity*: Planning agents are widely known. But there is also a need for instant reactions to changes in the environment. Therefore, they need perception capabilities (Franklin and Graesser 1997; Jennings and Wooldridge 1998).
- *Proactiveness*: The property of proactiveness is a counterpart of being reactive. Agents should reveal a goal-directed behavior and do something on their own initiative (Franklin and Graesser 1997; Jennings and Wooldridge 1998).

With respect to special intended usage areas, some more optional properties can be identified:

- *Adaptability*: Sometimes agents are characterized by their flexibility, adaptability, and facility to set up their own goals based on their implicit purpose (interests). One of the major characteristics of agents is their ability to acquire and process information about the situation, both spatially and temporally. That results in nonscripted actions (Franklin and Graesser 1997; Hayzelden and Bigham 1999).
- *Agent Granularity Degrees*: Agents may have degrees of complexity. Most simple agents are characterized by the lack of intelligence regarding their behavior. These agents are called reactive. More complex agents are called cognitive or intelligent agents. They are characterized by their ability to know their environment and to act on themselves and on the environment;

their observed behavior is a consequence of their perception, knowledge, and interactions (Hayzelden and Bigham 1999).

- *Learning*: Either the agency may perform some learning ability (as society) or each individual agent may be embedded with a learning algorithm (for example, a neural network or their reenforcement algorithm). Learning often allows the agent to alter its future action sequences and behavior such that future mistakes can be alleviated. Learning is often a factor that provides an agent with the ability to demonstrate adaptive behavior (Hayzelden and Bigham 1999).

- *Persistence*: An often required defined property is persistence. It describes the retention of identity and internal state for a longer period of time as a continuous process (Franklin and Graesser 1997; Jennings and Wooldridge 1998).

- *Collaboration*: A major characteristic of agent technology is the system decomposition into smaller, more specialized components. One drawback or advantage (depends on the viewpoint toward this characteristic) is that not every agent has the complete functionality to solve a problem. The needed interaction to reach the goals is collaboration (Jennings and Wooldridge 1998).

- *Mobility*: Another major advantage of agents is their ability to migrate between environments over a network (Franklin and Graesser 1997; Jennings and Wooldridge 1998). It is an extension of the client/server paradigm of computing by allowing the transmission of executable programs between client and server. Mobile agent usage can reduce network traffic and allow asynchronous interaction, disconnected operation, as well as remote searching and filtering. By this bandwidth, storage requirements may be positively impacted (DeTina and Poehlman 2002). Other fields of application are the access and administration of distributed information (Buraga 2003) or the dynamic configuration of an entity network (Sadiig 1997).

- *Character, Personality*: This property refers to a believable personality and an emotional state (Franklin and Graesser 1997; Jennings and Wooldridge 1998). So, it is describable within terms of an intentional stance in an anthropomorphic manner attributing to it beliefs and desires (DeTina and Poehlman 2002).

Another detailed overview about properties described in the literature is given in DeTina and Poehlman (2002). They list 21 properties according to the varying definitions of researchers (see Table 1.1).

1.5 CLASSIFICATIONS OF AGENTS

There exist several approaches with which to classify agents. A widely referenced approach is proposed by Franklin and Graesser (1997). For this purpose, they

TABLE 1.1
Properties of Agents

Property	A	B	C	D	E	F	G
Autonomy	*	*		*	*		*
Social Ability	*	*		*	*	*	*
Reactivity	*		*	*			
Proactiveness	*			*		*	
Mobility	*			*	*		
Veracity	*						
Benevolence	*						
Rationality	*		*				
Commitment		*					
Successful			*				
Capable/Competent			*			*	*
Perceptive			*			*	
Reflexive			*				
Predictive			*				
Interpretative			*				
Sound			*				
Temporally Continuous				*	*		
Ability to Learn				*			*
Flexible/Adaptable				*	*		
Character	*			*	*		*
Graceful Degradation							*

Source: DeTina, P. and W. F. S. Poehlman. 2002. Technical Report, McMaster University, Hamilton, Canada.
Notes: (A): Wooldridge, M. J. and N. R. Jennings. 1995. In *Intelligent Agents: Theories, Architectures, and Languages*, ed. M. J. Wooldridge, and N. R. Jennings, 1–39. New York: Springer. (B): Genesereth, M. R. 2004. Working Paper, Stanford University. http://logic.stanford.edu/kif/kif.html (accessed January 5, 2009). (C): Goodwin, R. 1993. Technical Report, School of Computer Science, Carnegie Mellon University, Pittsburgh, PA. (D): Franklin, S. and A. Graesser. 1997. In *Proceedings of the EACI Workshop on Agent Theories, Architectures, and Languages: Intelligent Agents III*, Lecture Notes in Artificial Intelligence, ed. M. J. Wooldridge and N. R. Jennings, 21–35. Berlin: Springer. (E): Etzioni, O. and D. S. Weld. 1995. *EEE Expert: Intelligent Systems and Their Applications* 10: 44–49. (F): Maes, P. 1996. *IEEE Expert: Intelligent Systems and Their Applications* 11: 62–63. (G): Foner, L. 1993. *What's An Agent, Anyway? A Sociological Case Study.* Cambridge, MA: MIT Press.

describe an initial "natural" taxonomy based on the same biological model as the classification of "living creatures." Figure 1.2 shows their approach.

Other classifying schemes may be based on, but are not limited to, the following:

- Tasks to be performed (e.g., information gathering, e-mail filtering)
- Control architecture (e.g., fuzzy subsumption agent, planning agent)

- Range and sensitivity of agents' senses
- Environment in which the agents are situated
- Communication complexity (e.g., discrete versus fully connected)
- Communication bandwidth
- Topology (by defining n properties and creating an n-dimensional matrix, each cell corresponds to a feature set that can be used as a classification category) (see Figure 1.3)

A taxonomy for Web agents was described in Huang et al. (2000). They also use a topology-based approach that encompasses text-based information retrieval agents as well as graphical avatars for user support. The authors focus on specific characteristics of used protocols (2D versus 3D), locality (client versus server), and the number of interacting agents (see Figure 1.4).

Sánchez bases his agent taxonomy on literature research regarding different views of agency focused on the term of agent autonomy (Sánchez 1997). Therefore, he distinguishes between the views toward agent technology as an abstraction to

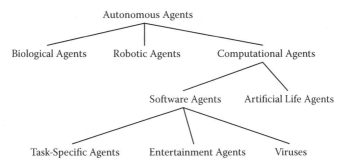

FIGURE 1.2 "Natural" taxonomy of agents. (Adapted from Franklin, S. and A. Graesser. 1997. In *Proceedings of the EACI Workshop on Agent Theories, Architectures, and Languages: Intelligent Agents III*, Lecture Notes in Artificial Intelligence, ed. M. J. Wooldridge and N. R. Jennings, 21–35. Berlin: Springer. With permission.)

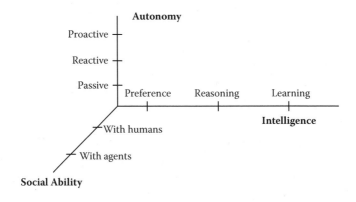

FIGURE 1.3 Chosen model of agent characteristics (see Darbyshire and Lowry 2000).

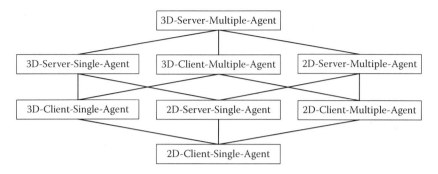

FIGURE 1.4 Lattice of Web agents (see Huang et al. 2000).

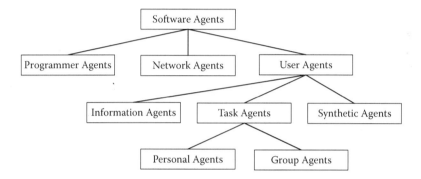

FIGURE 1.5 Agent taxonomy of Sánchez. (Adapted from Sánchez, J. A. 1997. A Taxonomy of Agents. Technical Report, Universidad de las Américas-Puebla, México. With permission.)

conceptualize, design, and implement complex systems (programmer agents); on the attribute of mobility (network agents); and on the view of end users as an abstraction to interact with systems. The latter classification of user agents is made from an application's point of view (see Figure 1.5).

Wong and Sycara (2000) presented a specialized taxonomy for what they call middle-agents, the agent-based connection between service-providing and service-requesting agents. Therefore, they defined six dimensions characterized by questions. The considered aspects are message sender type, information type, information processing type, information usage type, information processing type again, and the question of whether a middle-agent intermediates messages between service-requesting agents.

Another special taxonomy related to agent technology is described in Montaner, López, and De La Rosa (2003). After the analysis of 37 systems, they identified eight classes for recommender agents on the Internet. The classes in terms of profile exploitation are information filtering method, item-profile matching, and user-profile matching techniques. Following the aspect of profile generation and maintenance, there are the dimensions: the representation, the technique to generate the initial profile, the source of the relevance feedback that represents the user interest, the profile learning technique, and the profile adaptation technique.

Decker introduced a taxonomy with four dimensions as mentioned below (Decker 1987; Stone and Veloso 2003):

1. Agent granularity (coarse versus fine)
2. Heterogeneity of agent knowledge (redundant versus specialized)
3. Methods of distributing control (benevolent versus competitive, team versus hierarchical, static versus shifting roles)
4. Communication possibilities (blackboard versus messages, low-level versus high-level content)

An application-based classification was presented by Parunak (1996). The main characteristics were system function, agent architecture (degree of heterogeneity, reactive versus deliberative), and system architecture (communication, protocols, human involvement) (Stone and Veloso 2003).

Stone and Veloso argue that all aspects of agents are addressed by their heterogeneity/communication taxonomy (Stone and Veloso 2003). Based on literature research, they identified four agent classes: homogeneous noncommunicating agents, heterogeneous noncommunicating agents, homogeneous communicating agents, and heterogeneous communicating agents. These widespread classification approaches imply the already mentioned variety of views regarding agent technology.

1.6   BASIC AGENT ARCHITECTURES

An often asked question refers to the difference between the concepts of agents and objects as well as between agents and actors. Within the science of informatics, an object is described by the concepts of a class-instance relationship, inheritance, and message transmission. The first concept esteems a class as a model of structure and behavior, and an instance is seen as a concrete representation of the class. By inheritance, a class is derivable from another one and is thereby able to use its properties. Message transmission allows the definition of polymorphic procedures whose code can be variably interpreted by different clients. By these common concepts of objects, they cannot be interpreted as agents because they are not designed to fulfill certain goals or to satisfy a need. Furthermore, message transmission is only a procedure invocation (Ferber 1999). Agents are able to decide about message acceptance and about an appropriate reaction (see Figure 1.6).

Actors are parallel systems communicating by asynchronous buffered messages. They do not wait for an answer but order the receiver to send it to another actor. Actors are not agents due to the same reasons as explained above.

Agent architectures represent the transition from agent theory toward their practical application (Kernchen and Vornholt 2003). Therefore, three main research and application directions exist.

1.6.1   DELIBERATIVE AGENTS

Deliberative agents are based on classic artificial intelligence (AI) by explicitly requiring a symbolic model of the environment as well as the capability for logical

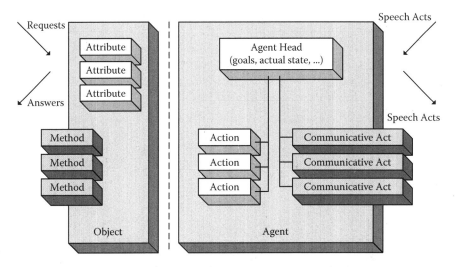

FIGURE 1.6 Comparison agent and object (see Ferber 1999; Bauer and Müller 2004).

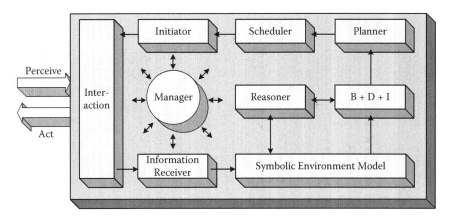

FIGURE 1.7 Deliberative agent architecture. (Adapted from Brenner, W., R. Zarnekow, and H. Wittig. 1998. *Intelligent Software Agents — Foundations and Applications* (German). Berlin: Springer. With permission.)

reasoning. Fundamental aspects are described by Newell and Simon within their "Physical-Symbol System Hypothesis" (Newell and Simon 1976). This theory describes a system being able to recognize symbols that can be combined to higher structures. An additional intention is its capability to run processes for symbol processing. The symbols can be used to create a symbolically encoded set of instructions. Their final statement is that such a system is capable of performing intelligent actions (see Figure 1.7).

Deliberative agents are the next step of this development. They contain an explicit symbolic model of the environment and decide following certain logical rules. The targeted types of problems to be solved include:

- *Transduction Problems*: Describing the translation of the real world into an adequate symbolic description.
- *Representation Problems*: Describing the symbolic representation of information about real-world objects and processes and how agents reason with those data.

The vision, especially of representatives of the classic AI, was to create automatic planning, automatic reasoning, and knowledge-based agents.

The most important deliberative architecture is the BDI Architecture of Rao and Georgeff (1991). It is exemplarily described below. The basic elements of this architecture are the *Beliefs, Desires,* and *Intentions*. They form the basis for the agent's capability for logical reasoning. Beliefs contain data about environmental information, action possibilities, capabilities, and resources. An agent must be able to manage the heterogeneous, changeable knowledge about the domain of its interest. The agent's desires derive from its beliefs and contain "individual" judgments of future environmental situations from the agent's point of view. The desires can be mutational, nonrealistic, and even come into conflict with each other. The intentions are a subset of the agent's actual goals and point to the goal that is actually intended to be achieved.

Additional components completing the mental state of a BDI agent are its goals and plans (Brenner, Zarnekow, and Wittig 1998). Goals are a subset of the agent's desires and describe its potential, realistic, not conflicting latitude. Plans subsume intentions and describe actions to solve a problem. The agent needs sensors to perceive data about its environment to create its world model (see Figure 1.8). These data need to be interpreted and may cause adaptations or an extension of the agent's actual beliefs. Actuators are used to realize plans with certain actions. Thereby, the agent changes its environment in a goal-directed, methodical way.

Because of the high complexity of appropriate environmental representations, deliberative agents are rarely sufficiently applicable within dynamic environments.

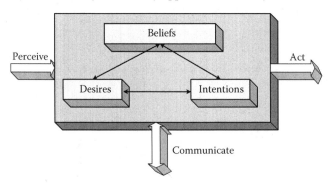

FIGURE 1.8   Beliefs, desires, and intentions (BDI) architecture (see Rao and Georgeff 1991).

1.6.2 REACTIVE AGENTS

Reactive agents are an alternative approach to solving problems that are not or only insufficiently solvable with symbolic AI. Therefore, a reactive agent architecture does not include an explicit description of the environment and mechanisms for logical reasoning.

Reactive agents perceive their environment and immediately react to occurring changes. This interaction is the basis for their intelligence, in contrast to the internal representations of deliberative agents (Brenner, Zarnekow, and Wittig 1998). The basic architecture of a reactive agent is shown in Figure 1.9. Even in complex situations, the agent only needs to identify basic axioms or dependencies. This information is processed by task-specific competence modules to create reactions. Again, actuators influence the environment based on the determined actions.

A representative of reactive agent architectures is the Subsumption Architecture (Brooks 1986). According to Brooks, every behavior is an almost independent process subsuming the behaviors of the lower behaviors (see Figure 1.10).

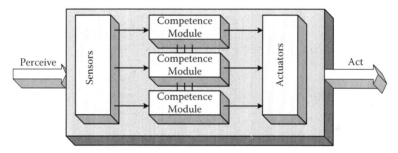

FIGURE 1.9 Reactive agent architecture (see Rao and Georgeff 1991).

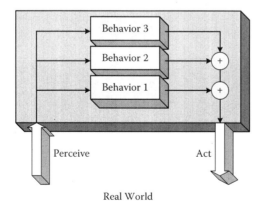

FIGURE 1.10 Subsumption agent architecture (see Brooks 1986).

1.6.3   HYBRID APPROACHES

Hybrid architectures try to combine different architectural approaches to a complex system. The idea behind them is to get all the advantages but none of the trade-offs of the particular approaches. Following Ferber (1999), hybrid approaches can be classified according to the capacity of agents to accomplish their tasks individually as well as to plan their actions (Figure 1.11).

In the literature, some authors, such as Brooks (1991), propose horizontal as well as vertical levels, each with its own functionality, in those complex systems. An example of a hybrid architecture, as developed by Müller in 1996, is shown in Figure 1.12.

One important advantage of agent technology is its possibility to find better solutions to problems due to the cooperation of many individuals. That directly leads to the concept of multiagent systems.

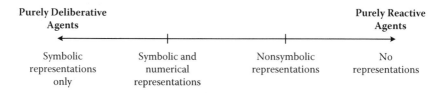

FIGURE 1.11   Hybrid agent architecture classification (see Ferber 1999).

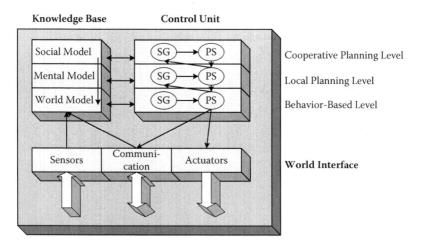

FIGURE 1.12   Hybrid agent architecture. (Adapted from Müller, J. P., M. Pischel, and M. Thiel. 1995. In *ECAI-94: Proceedings of the Workshop on Agent Theories, Architectures, and Languages on Intelligent Agents*, ed. M. J. Wooldridge and N. R. Jennings, 261–276. New York: Springer. With permission.)

1.7 MULTIAGENT SYSTEMS

The central approach of solving a given problem with a single agent may lead to certain restrictions (Nwana 1996; Sycara et al. 1996). Multiagent systems (MASs) are societies of a number of autonomous agents that work together to overcome them. MASs include autonomous agents' abilities and experiences as additional surplus value due to the interaction among individual agents, as this saying by Aristotle reflects: "The whole is more than the sum of its parts." Every agent of the MAS can either pursue its own goals and only communicate for information gathering or provide a coordinated, partial solution for the whole problem. But the agent always has a well-defined task that it is responsible and especially appropriate for.

Common areas of application are problem solving, multiagent simulation, the building of artificial worlds, collective robotics, and program design (Ferber 1999) (see Figure 1.13).

The term *multiagent system* (or MAS) is applied to a system including the following elements (Ferber 1999):

- An environment, E, that is a space that generally has a volume.
- A set of objects, O. These objects are situated; that is, it is possible at a given moment to associate any object with a position in E. These objects are passive; that is, they can be perceived, created, destroyed, and modified by the agents.
- An assembly of agents, A, that are specific objects ($A \subseteq O$) representing the active entities of the system.
- An assembly of relations, R, that link objects (and thus agents) to each other.

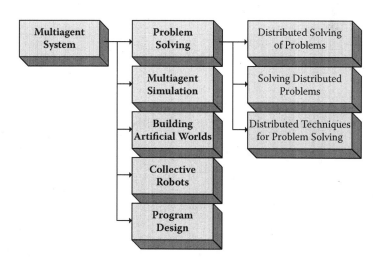

FIGURE 1.13 Classification of application types for multiagent systems (see Ferber 1999).

- An assembly of operations, Op, making it possible for the agents of A to perceive, produce, consume, transform, and manipulate objects from O.
- Operators with the task of representing the application of these operations and reactions of the world to this attempt at modification, which are called the laws of the universe.

MASs have several advantages (Hayzelden and Bigham 1999), as listed below:

- To address problems that are too large for a centralized single agent, for example because of resource limitations or for robustness concerns (the ability to recover from fault conditions or unexpected events).
- To enable the reduction of processing costs — it is less expensive (in hardware terms) to use a large number of inexpensive processors than a single processor with equivalent processing power.
- To allow for the interconnection and interoperation of multiple existing legacy systems, for example, expert systems, decision support systems, and legacy network protocols.
- To improve scalability — the organizational structure of the agents can dynamically change to reflect the dynamic environment — that is, as the network grows in size the agent organization can restructure by agents altering their roles, beliefs, and actions that they perform.
- To provide solutions to inherently distributed problems, for example, telecommunications control, air traffic control, and workflow management.
- To provide solutions that draw from distributed information sources.
- To provide solutions where the expertise is distributed.

Following (Brenner, Zarnekow, and Wittig 1998), the most important restrictions of single agents, and thereby reasons for the creation of MASs, include:

- An enormous amount of knowledge necessary for complex problems.
- The problem can be so complex that there exists no actual technology that enables one single agent to develop a solution.
- Many problems are distributed and require distributed solutions.
- Domain knowledge and other resources are often distributed among different places.
- Single agents can be bottlenecks in terms of processing speed, reliability, flexibility, and modularity.

An agent-based approach exists, which is different than multiagent systems, in that it is formed by subdividing system functionality. This layering architecture can have two occurrences: horizontal and vertical. In vertically layered agents, only the lowest layer senses the environment and only the highest layer acts. Here, a decomposition into subagents is unlikely. By contrast, horizontally layered agents can be decomposed, because each layer has sensing and acting functionalities (Müller, Pischel, and Thiel 1995).

1.8 AGENT INTERACTION

This concept is the basis for every successful society of agents. Without interaction, multiagent systems are only a set of individuals not being able to seize advantages out of the "multi" in "multiagent systems." Agent interaction describes a set of behaviors resulting from a society of agents that need to interact to reach their goals while considering possible limited resources and skills (Ferber 1999).

The most important aspects that design interaction of agents are their goals and intentions, available resources, and skills. Table 1.2 lists a typology of interaction situations.

MASs reveal an organizational structure characterized by an assembly of classes of agents (roles allocated to the agents) and a set of abstract relationships existing between these roles (see Ferber 1999). Five types of dimensions between organizations are visualized in Figure 1.14. Again, interaction is a key factor of this aspect of MASs and may result in fixed, variable, or evolutionary evolving couplings between organizational components:

1. The physical dimension (φ) describes nonvirtual existing aspects. That includes implementation and organizational architecture as well as its personal resources.
2. The social dimension (σ) is deduced from organizational theory and refers to role and place of the organization within a meta-organization.
3. The next dimension, the relational (α), is the most interesting one for agent interactions. It describes the exchanges that the organization might have with others on the same level, including communication and coordination.
4. As agents, organizations need capabilities to perceive reason and act with the environment. The environmental dimension (χ) is linked to that purpose.
5. Everything related to the organization is described in the personal dimension (ω).

TABLE 1.2
Classification of Interaction Situations

Goals	Resources	Skills	Type of Situation	Category
Compatible	Sufficient	Sufficient	*Independence*	Indifference
Compatible	Sufficient	Insufficient	*Simple collaboration*	Indifference
Compatible	Insufficient	Sufficient	*Obstruction*	Cooperation
Compatible	Insufficient	Insufficient	*Coordinated collaboration*	Cooperation
Incompatible	Sufficient	Sufficient	*Pure individual competition*	Cooperation
Incompatible	Sufficient	Insufficient	*Pure collective competition*	Antagonism
Incompatible	Insufficient	Sufficient	*Collective conflicts over resources*	Antagonism
Incompatible	Insufficient	Insufficient	*Collective conflicts over resources*	Antagonism

Source: Ferber, J. 1999. *Multi-Agent Systems — An Introduction to Distributed Artificial Intelligence.* New York: Addison Wesley. (With permission.)

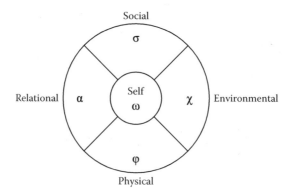

FIGURE 1.14 Aspects of analyzing organizations. (Adapted from Ferber, J. 1999. *Multi-Agent Systems — An Introduction to Distributed Artificial Intelligence.* New York: Addison Wesley. With permission.)

Following Brenner, Zarnekow, and Wittig (1998), the main aspects of agent interaction in MASs are communication and cooperation. Without these aspects, no mutual solution strategies can be developed and no distributed resources can be used. Thereby, the communication is the basis for cooperation.

1.8.1 COMMUNICATION

Communication is the foundation for every interaction. Its intentions are information and conversation. Agent communication theory is based on the theory of communication that emerged from telecommunications research (Shannon 1949). This model consists of a sender, who encodes the message to be sent with a language and sends it via a communication medium/channel to a receiver who decodes it. The situation that both sender and receiver are placed in is called the context of the communication (see Figure 1.15).

The differences between communication of objects and agents are already described in Section 1.6 and Figure 1.6. The most basic communication method of agents is a procedure call, where the message is encoded within the parameters and the answer is the return value of the procedure. But with this, only primitive communication can be established. Blackboard and message-based communications are more appropriate techniques and are described below.

1.8.1.1 Blackboard Technique for Communication

A *blackboard* is a shared working environment for all participating agents to share information, data, and knowledge (Brenner, Zarnekow, and Wittig 1998).

Its origins lie within the research of distributed AI. To communicate, an agent writes information on the blackboard — the message is *sent*. To *receive* a message, an agent reads (potentially filtered) information from the blackboard. No direct communication between agents is established. For management and security purposes, a central management component can be included, where agents need to register themselves. Multiple specialized blackboards can exist within an MAS and, additionally,

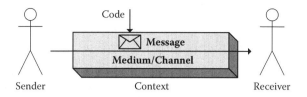

FIGURE 1.15 Classic model of communication theory (see Ferber 1999).

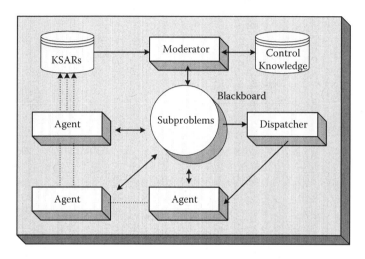

FIGURE 1.16 Extended blackboard structure. (Adapted from Brenner, W., R. Zarnekow, and H. Wittig. 1998. *Intelligent Software Agents — Foundations and Applications* (German). Berlin: Springer. With permission.)

one agent may register for more than one blackboard. Figure 1.16 visualizes an extended blackboard architecture that includes the already mentioned management component, a dispatcher for agent notification, and further refined mechanisms for knowledge access (knowledge source activation record, [KSAR]).

An MAS may consist of hundreds or thousands of agents being distributed across an unreliable network; then communication based on a shared memory is not always a sufficient solution for message exchange (Tanenbaum and van Steen 2002). Other communication approaches are needed.

1.8.1.2 Messages and Conversations for Communication

Communication based on message exchange provides a flexible basis for complex scenarios (Brenner, Zarnekow, and Wittig 1998). It has its foundations in speech act theory based on the research of Austin (2005), Searle (1969), and Habermas (1984). Five types of speech acts exist (Schoop 2001; Searle 1969), and each has a locutionary aspect describing its physical creation, an illocutionary aspect describing the sender's intention, and a perlocutionary aspect describing the effects of the speech act at the side of the receiver (Austin 2005):

- *Assertive Speech Act*: Express facts about the world.
- *Directive Speech Act*: Express instructions for the receiver.
- *Commissive Speech Act*: Express the sender's commitment for future actions.
- *Expressive Speech Act*: Express the sender's feelings or psychological attitudes.
- *Declarative Speech Act*: Express how the world is changed due to the speech act.

Message-based communication follows the structure presented in Figure 1.15. The message structure is defined by certain agent communication languages (ACLs) for a free content composition. Based on these degrees of freedom, extremely complex and flexible dialogues can be defined. ACLs, conversations, and some protocols as generally accepted dialogue structures are described below.

1.8.1.3   Agent Communication Languages

Following Ferber (1999), a communication language is one of the four basic languages for agent technology implementation. The others refer to the implementation and formalization of multiagent systems, to the knowledge representation of agents, as well as to the definition of behavior. Figure 1.17 shows these aspects.

Communication languages (type L2) are thereby used for data transmission and mutual requests for information and services. Their efficient usage is the basis for all interaction types, and by this, advantages are inherited in multiagent systems. KQML is the classic referenced language. Other languages are as follows:

- *Implementation Languages (type L1)*: Are used to program agents and agent-based systems.
- *Behavior Description Languages (type L3)*: Prescribed from implementation and are necessary to describe additional details to understand the environment and the behavior of agents.
- *Knowledge Representation Languages (type L4)*: Are used to model information about the environment and to deduce assumptions about the future.
- *Specification Languages (type L5)*: Define a common understanding of multiagent systems based on certain concepts as well as determine requirements for the modeling and implementation of those systems.

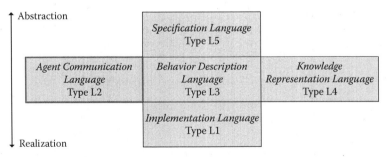

FIGURE 1.17   Agent communication language in the context of other implementation languages. (Adapted from Ferber, J. 1999. *Multi-Agent Systems — An Introduction to Distributed Artificial Intelligence*. New York: Addison Wesley. With permission.)

TABLE 1.3

Common Agent Communication Languages

Agent Communication Language	Language Characteristic
ACML	XML-based
Agent-0	KQML-based
AgenTalk	Descriptive language
April++	OO concurrent language
COOL	Descriptive language
DIAGAL	Descriptive language
FIPA-ACL	XML-based
FLBC	XML-based
GroupLog	Extended Horn clauses
JADL	Java-based
KIF	Descriptive language
KLAIM	Descriptive language
KQML	Descriptive language
Little-JIL	Visual language
LuCe	Prolog-related
MAI^{2}L	Descriptive language
sACL	Command language
Telescript	Command language
TRUCE	Protocol specification
WARREN-ACL	KQML-based
3APL	Command language

Source: Revised and extended version of Wille (2005).

All of these types of languages are connected to each other, for example, a representative of L2 is used to send a message that can be interpreted by a representative of L3.

Table 1.3 gives an overview of existing agent communication languages and is based on the literature (Barbuceanu and Lo 2000; Bryce and Cremonini 2001; Chaib-draa et al. 2006; Cockayne and Zyda 1997; FIPA00061 2002; Freeman, Hupfer, and Arnold 1999; Garcia, Lucena, and Cowan 2004; Genesereth 2004; Grosof and Labrou 2000; Haugeneder and Steiner 1998; Hendriks et al. 2000; Jeon, Petrie, and Cutkosky 2000; Kuwabara, Ishida, and Osato 1995; Labrou and Finin 1997; Liu and Ye 2001; Moore 2000; Papadopoulos 2001; Petrie 2001; Pitt and Mamdani 2000; Rossi, Cabri, and Denti 2001; Skarmeas 1999).

KQML (Knowledge Query Manipulation Language) (Labrou and Finin 1997) and FIPA-ACL (Foundation for Intelligent Physical Agents/Agent Communication Language) (FIPA00061 2002) are the two main agent languages (Chaib-draa et al. 2006). Both are based on the speech act theory.

KQML and FIPA-ACL treat messages as environment-influencing actions, and their message types are named *performatives*. KQML was developed in the context of DARPA (Defense Advanced Research Projects Agency) research (Chaib-draa et al. 2006). A corresponding message has three conceptual levels:

1. *Communication level* to specify sender and receiver.
2. *Message level* to specify performative, knowledge representation language, and used ontology.
3. Content *level* to specify the message's content.

Some performatives of KQML are categorized in Table 1.4.

Notice that a later definition of semantic for KQML messages was proposed (Labrou and Finin 1998). Certain KQML and FIPA-ACL messages might reveal a similar structure due to the same theoretical fundamentals and the same intentional usage, as well as due to their mutual development. A KQML message has the following structure:

```
(KQML-performative
        :sender <word>
        :receiver <word>
        :language <word>
        :ontology <word>
        :content <expression> ... )
```

KQML was not sufficient for researchers and practitioners due to several reasons. First, problems were the imprecise definition of the performatives and their large,

---

TABLE 1.4

Classification of Knowledge Query Manipulation Language (KQML) Performatives

Function Class	Member Performatives	Level
Query and response	Ask-if, ask-all, ask-about, ask-one, tell, untell, deny, sorry	Agent-pair
Cursor manipulation and result formatting	Ready, next, discard, rest stream-all, stream-about, eos	Agent-pair
Advertise or commit to a capability	Advertise, unadvertise	Agent community
KB editing	Insert, uninsert, delete-one, delete-all, undelete	Agent-pair
Enactment	Achieve, unachieve	Agent-pair
Error handling	Error	Agent-pair
Communication primitives other than pure asynchronous messages	Broadcast, forward, standby, subscribe and monitor (like a kb alerter), pipe, break (make and dismantle a pipe), generator	Either
Trading	Broker-one, broker-all, recommend-one, recommend-all, recruit-one, recruit-all	Agent-community
Name service	Register, unregister, transport-address	Agent-community

Source: Vasudevan, V. 1998. Technical Report, Object Services and Consulting Inc. www.objs.com (accessed January 5, 2009).

almost not handable and not-bounded number. The interaction of different MAS implementations was not always guaranteed. Additionally, no protocol for message transport was specified and no semantics of the language were defined. Also, some performatives for action coordination were missing.

As a result of interoperability, communication and message transport were not supported to a usable extent. So, FIPA-ACL was developed. FIPA-ACL is a standard that defines messages and their descriptions that are intended to be used for agent communication. It differs from KQML in the available performatives and in the defined semantics.

For the second point, a Semantic Language (SL) was developed to model beliefs, vague beliefs, and desires of agents (Wooldridge 2002). SL defines feasibility conditions and rational effects for every performative. The SL-based semantic definition of the *inform-performative* is (FIPA00037 2002):

$< i, \text{inform}(j, \varphi) >$
- Feasibility precondition: $B_{i\varphi} \wedge \neg B(Bif_{j\varphi} \vee Uif_{j\varphi})$
- Rational effect: $B_{i\varphi}$

A corresponding message contains the mandatory parameter *performative* (FIPA00037 2002) for a list of available performatives and several other optional parameters (see Table 1.5).

TABLE 1.5

Foundation for Intelligent Physical Agents/Agent Communication Language (FIPA-ACL) Message Parameters

Parameter	Category of Parameter
performative	Type of communicative act
sender	Participant in communication
receiver	Participant in communication
reply-to	Participant in communication
content	Content of message
language	Description of content
encoding	Description of content
ontology	Description of content
protocol	Control of conversation
conversation-id	Control of conversation
reply-with	Control of conversation
in-reply-to	Control of conversation
reply-by	Control of conversation

Source: FIPA00037 2002. FIPA Communicative Act Library Specification SC00037J. Standard Document, Geneva: FIPA Organization.

An exemplary FIPA-ACL message has the following structure:

```
(inform
        :sender agent1
        :reveiver agent2
        :content (price good2 150)
        :language sl
        :ontology hpl-auction
        )
```

Communication between agents can result in extended message sequences, also called conversation or dialogue. Walton and Krabbe (1995) list several types of conversation. They are presented in Table 1.6.

Often, occurring conversation patterns are specified for common agreement. Some chosen generally accepted and standardized protocols include (Pitt and Mamdani 2000):

- Contract-Net Protocol
- Yes-No-Query Protocol
- Confirmation Protocol
- Haggle Protocol
- Commitment Protocol
- FIPA Conversation Protocols (e.g., FIPA Iterated Contract Net Interaction Protocol Specification [FIPA00061 2002] and other FIPA Standard protocols)
- Request-for-Action Protocol (Winograd and Flores 1986)

Protocols with a large number of states can become crucial for agent communication because of possible computation problems as well as due to its decreased flexibility for agents (Chaib-draa et al. 2006).

TABLE 1.6
Primary Types of Dialogue

Type of Dialogue	Goal of the Dialogue	Initial Situation
Persuasion	Resolution of conflict	Conflicting point of view
Negotiation	Making a deal	Conflict of interest
Deliberation	Reaching a decision	Need for action
Information seeking	Spreading knowledge	Personal ignorance
Inquiry	Growth of knowledge	General ignorance
Eristic	Accommodation in relationship	Antagonism

Source: Walton, D. N. and E. C. W. Krabbe. 1995. *Commitment in Dialogue: Basic Concepts of Interpersonal Reasoning*. New York: State University of New York Press.

1.8.2 AGENT COOPERATION

Especially in environments with a lot of cooperation between participants, agent technology can map emerging requirements and patterns because of the ability of participants to cooperate (Kargl, Illmann, and Weber 1999). This cooperation between entities can be the largest context of interaction (Dumke, Koeppe and Wille 2000). Mentionable aspects of this activity are the coordination of actions, the degree of parallelism, the sharing of resources, system robustness, the nonredundancy of actions, as well as the nonpersistence of conflicts. Cooperation indicators are increasing individual and group survival capacity, performance improvement, and conflict resolution. Therefore, a usual definition of cooperation is given as by Ferber (1999). There cooperation is collaboration, coordination of actions, and the resolution of conflicts.

Cooperation is mainly implemented for several reasons. This includes the reduction of communication costs that are associated with a central problem solver, the improvement of performance through parallelism, increased reactivity because it is not necessary to consult a central problem solver, and improved robustness by reduced dependencies (Hayzelden and Bigham 1999). Therefore, the addition of new agents should lead to increased performance of the group, and their performed actions should solve or avoid actual or potential conflicts (Ferber 1999). Cooperation methods are classifiable into six categories (Ferber 1999). Correlating problems, techniques, and objectives are visualized in Figure 1.18:

- *Grouping and Multiplication*: Grouping is a natural phenomenon that describes a more or less homogeneous unit that emerges from physical closeness or the existence of a communication network. It is the basis for specialization and supports learning. Multiplication includes several advantages in situations that benefit from pure quantity of individuals, resources, or skills. Overall performance and reliability can be increased without an increase in individual productivity.
- *Communication*: This aspect is the base of every other cooperation. It connects the individuals of the agent society either by explicit messages or signals in the environment.
- *Specialization*: Specialization is a process of adaptation toward specific tasks. This special performance increase has as a trade-off the decreased ability to perform other tasks. In this case, multiple individuals in a group are needed for multiple jobs to be performed for an overall task.
- *Collaborating by Sharing Tasks and Resources*: Collaboration is one of the intentions of communication. It requires a general goal to be achieved. To keep it, a distributed allocation of tasks, information, and resources is needed (Dumke, Koeppe, and Wille 2000).
- *Coordination of Actions*: Coordination in MASs is needed due to reasons including prevention from confusion, the meeting of global constraints, specialty of agents, and depending subactions (Hayzelden and Bigham

1999). Mainly, the reasons evolve from the fact of a missing global view on the complete problem. They need further information and services to obtain solutions to the local problem that are intended to subsume that solutions to the global problem. That needs to be arranged in a reasonable way. Coordination can be achieved by synchronization, planning, reaction, and regulation.

- *Conflict Resolution by Arbitration and Negotiation*: These two approaches are used to minimize reduction of system performance due to conflicts between individual agents. Arbitrations lead to behavioral rules whose concern is to restrict conflicts and preserve the society of agents.

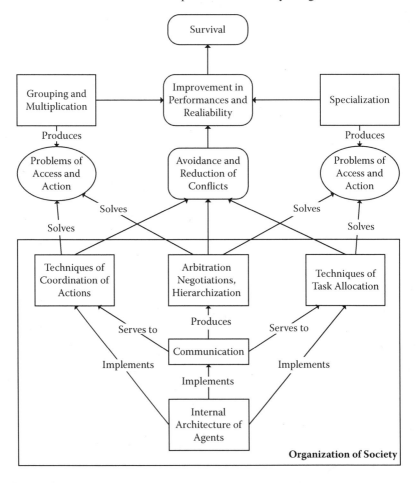

FIGURE 1.18 Characteristics of cooperation in agent-based organizations. (Adapted from Ferber, J. 1999. *Multi-Agent Systems — An Introduction to Distributed Artificial Intelligence.* New York: Addison Wesley. With permission.)

The following section will briefly define the main parts of cooperation following Ferber.

1.8.2.1 Collaboration

Agents collaborate, when they are working together. Collaboration techniques are those that distribute tasks, information, and resources among agents in the advancement of a common labor. Such a distribution can be centralized by coordination agents or decentralized by offering supplies and demands. Distributed approaches may be based on the market principle or on mutual representations of the agents' capacities (Ferber 1999). In summary, collaboration is the collective solution of a problem or the collection processing of a task by a society of agents.

The addressed advantages of agent collaboration, such as increased processing speed and robustness, are "paid" for by trade-offs related to overheads in terms of team formation and collaboration, agent communication, and team maintenance (Wilsker 1996). Some exemplary multiagent collaboration strategies include:

- Joint Intentions model of Cohen and Levesque (Cohen and Lesvesque 1990, 1991)
- SharedPlan Model of Collaboration (Grosz and Sidner 1990)
- Planned Team Activity by Kinny (Kinny et al. 1994)
- Commitment Based on Agents' Mental States and Relationships by Castelfranchi (1995)
- Responsibility Delegation by Matsubayashi (Matsubayashi and Tokoro 1993)
- Team Formation by Tidhar (Tidhar et al. 1992)

1.8.2.2 Coordination

Coordination is the next part of interaction following Ferber's widely accepted definition. Main research and definition approaches are based on, among others, Malone and Crowston (1994), Wegner (1996), and Gelernter and Carriero (1992).

In summary, coordination is the management of interaction and dependencies between certain agents (Omicini 2001).

Coordination techniques can be classified (Nwana, Lee, and Jennings 1997) as follows:

- *Organizational Structuring* by defining an interaction framework with roles, communication paths, and authority relationships.
- *Contracting* by using manager agents for problem decomposition and task assignment.
- *Multiagent Planning* by a centralized or distributed planning of interaction to avoid conflicting actions.
- *Negotiation* by interaction to reach a mutually accepted agreement.

Within coordination techniques and strategies, agents may serve as coordination components (Papadopoulos 2001). A corresponding approach is a facilitator/mediator where the agent provides services and thereby satisfies the requests of other agents. Broker agents also satisfy requests, but by providing third-party services. A special look-up service (yellow pages) is provided by matchmaker agents. Repository agents managing requests for other agents follow the blackboard approach. The management and conduction of communication for other agents in a well-defined area leads to a job description of a local area coordinator agent. Cooperation domain servers are agents providing facilities to access shared information and to subscribe and exchange messages.

1.8.2.3 Conflict Resolution

Classically, conflicts are seen as disturbances within MASs (Tessier, Chaudron, and Müller 2001). On a conceptual level, resource conflicts and knowledge conflicts exist. The first type can occur when a resource, like processing time, is involved. Knowledge conflicts arise when the agents' information differ. Contradiction between propositions is most dealt with.

Following Tessier, Chaudron, and Müller (2001), a conflict is a subset of all propositional attitudes (for example, beliefs, desires, intentions, hopes, and so forth) of the agent that must be reduced by removing a propositional attitude.

In other words, it is a situation with incompatible or exclusive attitudes. Appropriate approaches try to anticipate, solve, or avoid them; otherwise, conflicts remain unsolved and change agents' behavior or enrich agents' knowledge. Following Aimeur (2001), the three modes for conflict resolution include:

1. *Negotiation*: As a discussion procedure to reach a common agreement between the involved parties.
2. *Mediation*: As a negotiation with a neutral party that facilitates the solution research.
3. *Arbitration*: As the decision of a solution by a neutral party.

In summary, conflict resolution is the application of certain techniques for the transition from a situation with conflicting agent attitudes to a situation with less or no conflicting agent attitudes.

1.8.3 Agent Mobility

Another major advantage of agents is their ability to migrate between environments over a network (Franklin and Graesser 1997; Jennings and Wooldridge 1998). It is an extension of the client/server paradigm of computing by allowing the transmission of executable programs between network nodes (see Figure 1.19).

So, agent mobility is the agent's property that permits the continuation of its execution on another network node other than where it was started (OMG 2000). Mobile agent usage can reduce network traffic, overcome network latency, and allow asynchronous and autonomous interactions, disconnected operation (see Figure 1.20),

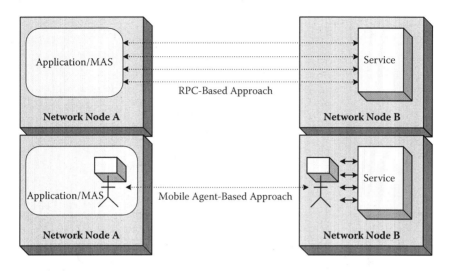

FIGURE 1.19 Mobile agent paradigm (see Lange and Oshima 1998).

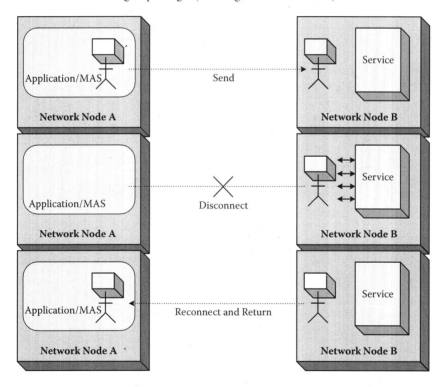

FIGURE 1.20 Disconnected operation (see Lange and Oshima 1998).

as well as remote searching and filtering. Furthermore, they encapsulate protocols, adapt dynamically, are naturally heterogeneous and robust, and are fault tolerant (Lange and Oshima 1998).

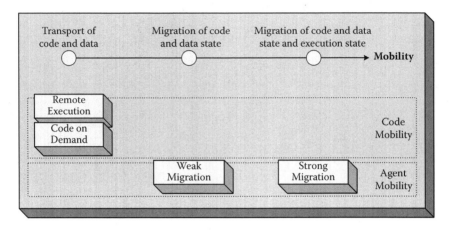

FIGURE 1.21   Agent mobility (see Grasshopper 2004).

Due to this, bandwidth and storage requirements may be positively impacted (DeTina and Poehlman 2002). Other fields of application are the access and administration of distributed information (Buraga 2003) or the dynamic configuration of an entity network (Sadiig 1997). Additional useful implementations are related to remote diagnostics, maintenance, control, or other related services for stationary or mobile technical systems (Jain, Che, and Ichalkaranje 2002).

The standard for agent mobility, Mobile Agent System Interoperability Facility (MASIF), was proposed by the Object Management Group (OMG). It standardizes agent management, agent transfer, agent and agent system names, as well as agent system type and location syntax (OMG 2000).

Several types of agent mobility can be distinguished. One is related to an agent's execution state. Thereby, strong migration means the agent is migrated together with its execution state. It carries all stack information about which one to determine the point of task execution. Weak migration only supports the transport of predefined data (see Figure 1.21).

Societies of agents are often logically fragmented for the semantic aggregation of single but related agents. These cities or regions accommodate certain agents. The migration of agents from one region to another within the same agent platform is named *intraplatform migration*. Its counterpart is interplatform migration.

REFERENCES

Aimeur, E. 2001. Strategic Use of Conflicts in Tutoring Systems. In *Conflicting Agents: Conflict Management in Multi-Agent Systems*, ed. C. Tessier, L. Chaudron, and H. Müller, 223–250. Boston: Kluwer Academic.

Anghel, C. and I. Salomie. 2003. JADE Based Solutions for Knowledge Assessment in eLearning Environments. Working Paper, JADE Research Center. http://jade.tilab.com/papers/EXP/Anghel.pdf (accessed January 5, 2009).

Austin, J. L. 2005. *How to Do Things with Words*. Cambridge: Harvard University Press.

Barbuceanu, M. and W. Lo 2000. Conversation-Oriented Programming for Agent Interaction. In *Issues in Agent Communication*, ed. F. Dignum and M. Greaves, 220–234. Berlin: Springer.

Bauer, B. and J. P. Müller. 2004. Using UML in the Context of Agent-Oriented Software Engineering: State of the Art. In *Agent-Oriented Software Engineering IV*, ed. P. Giorgini, J. P. Müller, and J. Odell, 1–24. Berlin: Springer.

Brenner, W., R. Zarnekow, and H. Wittig. 1998. *Intelligent Software Agents — Foundations and Applications* (German). Berlin: Springer.

Brooks, R. A. 1986. A Robust Layered Control System for a Mobile Robot. *IEEE Journal of Robotics and Automation*, Vol. RA-2: 14–23.

Brooks, R. A. 1991. Intelligence without Representation. In *Proceedings of the 12th International Joint Conference on Artificial Intelligence* (IJCAI-91), ed. R. Reiter and J. Myopoulos, 569–595. San Francisco, CA: Morgan Kaufmann.

Bryce, C. and M. Cremonini. 2001. Coordination and Security on the Internet. In *Coordination of Internet Agents Models, Technologies, and Applications*, ed. A. Omincini, F. Zambonelli, M. Klusch, and R. Tolksdorf, 274–298. Berlin: Springer.

Buraga, S. C. 2003. Developing Agent-Oriented E-Learning Systems. In *Proceedings of the 14th International Conference on Control Systems and Computer Science*, ed. I. Dumitrache and C. Buiu, Bucharest: Polytehnica Press.

Caire, G., F. Garijo, F. Leal, P. Chainho, and P. Massonet. 2001. PIR4.3: Case Study Development. Technical Report, EURESCOM Project P907, University of Madrid, Spain.

Castelfranchi, C. 1995. Commitments: From Individual Intentions to Groups and Organizations. In *Proceedings of the First International Conference on Multiagent Systems*, ed. V. R. Lesser and L. Gasser, 41–48. Cambridge, MA: MIT Press.

Chaib-draa, B., M. Labrie, M. Bergeron, and P. Pasquier. 2006. DIAGAL: An Agent Communication Language Based on Dialogue Games and Sustained by Social Commitments. *Autonomous Agents and Multi-Agent Systems* 13: 61–95.

Chainho, P., P. Massonet, F. Garijo, J. G. Sanz, J. Pavon, G. Caire, F. Leal, and J. Stark. 2000. Analysis of the UPA Case Study (PIR4.2 Case Study 1 B1). Technical Report, EURESCOM Project P907, University of Madrid, Spain.

Cockayne, W. and M. Zyda. 1997. *Mobile Agents*. Greenwich, CT: Manning.

Cohen, P. R. and H. J. Levesque. 1990. Intention Is Choice with Commitment. *Artificial Intelligence* 43: 213–261.

Cohen, P. R. and H. J. Levesque. 1991. Confirmations and Joint Action. In *Proceedings of the 12th International Joint Conference on Artificial Intelligence* (IJCAI'1991), ed. J. Mylopoulos and R. Reiter, 951–959. San Francisco, CA: Morgan Kaufman.

Darbyshire, P. and G. Lowry. 2000. An Overview of Agent Technology and Its Application to Subject Management. In *Proceedings of the IRMA International Conference, Anchorage*, 509–512. Los Altimos, CA: IEEE Computer Society Press.

Decker, K. S. 1987. Distributed Problem Solving: A Survey. *IEEE Transactions on Systems, Man, and Cybernetics* 17: 729–740.

DeTina, P. and W. F. S. Poehlman. 2002. DISTRIBUTED SYSTEMS II — A Survey of Software Agent Attributes. Technical Report, McMaster University, Hamilton, Canada.

Dumke, R., R. Koeppe, and C. Wille. 2000. Software Agent Measurement and Self-Measuring Agent-Based Systems. Preprint No. 11, Department of Computer Science, University of Magdeburg, Germany.

Etzioni, O. and D. S. Weld. 1995. Intelligent Agents on the Internet: Fact, Fiction, and Forecast. *EEE Expert: Intelligent Systems and Their Applications* 10: 44–49.

Ferber, J. 1999. *Multi-Agent Systems — An Introduction to Distributed Artificial Intelligence*. New York: Addison Wesley.

FIPA00023 2002. FIPA Agent Management Specification SC00023J. Standard Document, Geneva: FIPA Organization. www.fipa.org (accessed January 5, 2009).

FIPA00037 2002. FIPA Communicative Act Library Specification SC00037J. Standard Document, Geneva: FIPA Organization.

FIPA00061 2002. FIPA ACL Message Structure Specification SC00061G. Standard Document, Geneva: FIPA Organization.

Foner, L. 1993. *What's An Agent, Anyway? A Sociological Case Study.* Cambridge, MA: MIT Press.

Franklin, S. and A. Graesser. 1997. Is It an Agent, or Just a Program?: A Taxonomy for Autonomous Agents. In *Proceedings of the EACI Workshop on Agent Theories, Architectures, and Languages: Intelligent Agents III*, Lecture Notes in Artificial Intelligence, ed. M. J. Wooldridge and N. R. Jennings, 21–35. Berlin: Springer.

Freeman, E., S. Hupfer, and K. Arnold. 1999. *JavaSpaces — Principles, Patterns, and Practice.* New York: Addison Wesley.

Garcia, A. F., C. J. P. Lucena, and D. D. Cowan. 2004. Agents in Object-Oriented Software Engineering. *Software-Practice and Experience* 34(5): 489–521.

Gelernter, D. and N. Carriero. 1992. Coordination Languages and Their Significance. *Communications of the ACM* 35: 97–107.

Genesereth, M. R. 2004. *Knowledge Interchange Language.* Working Paper, Stanford University. http://logic.stanford.edu/kif/kif.html (accessed January 5, 2009).

Goodwin, R. 1993. Formalizing Properties of Agents. Technical Report, School of Computer Science, Carnegie Mellon University, Pittsburgh, PA.

Grasshopper 2004. Grasshopper 2 Agent Platform. Working Paper, cordis.europa.eu/infowin/acts/analysis/products/thematicalagents/ch4/ch4.htm (accessed January 5, 2009).

Grosof, B. N. and Y. Labrou. 2000. An Approach to Using XML and Rule-Based Content Languages with an Agent Communication Language. In *Issues in Agent Communication*, ed. F. Dignum and M. Greaves, 96–117. Berlin: Springer.

Grosz, B. and C. Sidner. 1990. Plans for Discourse. In *Intentions in Communication*, ed. P. R. Cohen, J. Morgan, and M. A. Pollack, 417–444. Cambrige, MA: MIT Press.

Habermas, J. 1984. *The Theory of Communicative Action — Reason and the Rationalization of Society.* Oxford: Butterworth-Heinemann.

Haugeneder, H. and D. Steiner. 1998. Co-Operating Agents: Concepts and Applications. In *Agent Technology — Foundation, Application, and Markets*, ed. N. R. Jennings, and M. J. Wooldridge, 175–202. Berlin: Springer.

Hayzelden, A. L. G. and J. Bigham. 1999. Agent Technology in Communications Systems: An Overview. *Knowledge Engineering Review* 14: 341–375.

Hendriks, K. V., F. S. de Boer, W. van der Hoek, and J. J. C. Meyer. 2000. Semantics of Communication Agents Based on Deduction and Abduction. In *Issues in Agent Communication*, ed. F. Dignum and M. Greaves, 63–79. Berlin: Springer.

Huang, Z., A. Eliens, A. van Ballegooij, and P. de Bra. 2000. A Taxonomy of Web Agents. In *Proceedings of the 11th International Workshop on Database and Expert Systems Applications* (DEXA'00), ed. D. Stamoulis and P. Gerogiadis, Los Altimos, CA: IEEE Computer Press.

Jafari, A. 2002. Conceptualizing Intelligent Agents for Teaching and Learning. *EQ Educause Quaterly* 3: 28–34.

Jain, L. C., Z. Chen, and N. Ichalkaranje. 2002. *Intelligent Agents and Their Applications.* Heidelberg: Physica.

Jennings, N. R. and M. J. Wooldridge. 1998. *Agent Technology — Foundation, Applications and Markets.* Berlin: Springer.

Jeon, H., C. Petrie, and M. R. Cutkosky. 2000. JATLite: A Java Agent Infrastructure with Message Routing. *IEEE Internet Computer* 4(2): 87–96.

Kargl, F., T. Illmann, and M. Weber. 1999. CIA — A Collaboration and Coordination Infrastructure for Personal Agents. In *Proceedings of the IFIP WG 6.1 International Working Conference on Distributed Applications and Interoperable* Systems II (DAIS 1999), ed. L. Kutonen, H. König, and M. Tienan, 213–318. Boston: Kluwer Academic.

Kearney, P., J. Stark, F. Leal, and J. P. Rodrigues. 2000. Analysis of the ACSOSS Case Study (PIR 4.2 B.0). Technical Report, EURESCOM Project P907, University of Madrid, Spain.

Kernchen, S. 2004. Evaluation of ALIVE — Implemented with the Grasshopper Technology (Case study in German), Working Paper, Department of Computer Science, University of Magdeburg, Germany.

Kernchen, S. and S. Vornholt. 2003. The Agent-Based System ALIVE. Working Paper, Department of Computer Science, University of Magdeburg, Germany.

Kinny, D., M. Ljungberg, A. S. Rao, L. Sonenberg, G. Tidhar, and E. Werner. 1994. Planned Team Activity. In *MAAMAW '92: Selected Papers from the Fourth European Workshop on Modelling Autonomous Agents in a Multi-Agent World, Artificial Social Systems*, ed. A. Colonies, C. Castelfranchi, and E. Werner, 227–256. Berlin: Springer.

Kuwabara, K., T. Ishida, and N. Osato. 1995. AgenTalk: Coordination Protocol Description for Multiagent Systems. In *Proceedings of the First International Conference on Multiagent Systems*, ed. V. R. Lesser and L. Gasser, Cambridge, MA: MIT Press.

Labrou, Y. and T. Finin. 1997. A Proposal for a New KQML Specification. Working Paper, University of Maryland, www.cs.umbc.edu/kqml/papers/ (accessed January 5, 2009).

Labrou, Y. and T. Finin. 1998. Semantics and Conversations for an Agent Communication Language. In *Readings in Agents,* ed. M. N. Huhns and M. P. Singh, 235–242. San Francisco, CA: Morgan Kaufmann.

Lange, D. B. and M. Oshima. 1998. *Programming and Developing JAVA Mobile Agents with Aglets*. Reading, MA: Addison-Wesley.

Liu, J. and Y. Ye. 2001. *E-Commerce Agents — Marketplace Solutions, Security Issues, and Supply and Demand*. LNAI 2033, Berlin: Springer.

Maes, P. 1994. Agents That Reduce Work and Information Overload. *Communications of the ACM* 37(7): 30–40.

Maes, P. 1996. Intelligent Software: Easing the Burdens That Computers Put on People. *IEEE Expert: Intelligent Systems and Their Applications* 11: 62–63.

Malone, T. W. and K. Crowston. 1994. The Interdisciplinary Study of Coordination. *ACM Computing Surveys* 26: 87–119.

Markham, S., J. Ceddia, J. Sheard, C. Burvill, J. Weir, B. Field, L. Sterling, and L. Stern. 2003. Applying Agent Technology to Evaluation Tasks in e-Learning Environments. In *Proceedings of the Exploring Educational Technologies Conference*, ed. C. Burvill and J. Weir, 1–7. Melbourne: University Press.

Matsubayashi, K. and M. Tokoro. 1993. A Collaboration Mechanism on Positive Interactions in Multi-Agent Environments. In *Proceedings of the 13th International Joint Conference on Artificial Intelligence (IJCAI 1993)*, ed. R. Bajcsy, 346–351. New York: Springer.

Milgrom, E., P. Chainho, Y. Deville, R. Evans, P. Kearney, and P. Massonet. 2001. MESSAGE — Methodology for Engineering Systems of Software Agents. Technical Report, EURESCOM Project P907, University of Madrid, Spain.

Montaner, M., B. López, and J. L. De La Rosa. 2003. A Taxonomy of Recommender Agents on the Internet. *Artificial Intelligence Review* 19(4): 285–330.

Moore, S. A. 2000. On Conversation Policies and the Need for Exceptions. In *Issues in Agent Communication*, ed. F. Dignum and M. Greaves, 144–159. Berlin: Springer.

Müller, J. P., M. Pischel, and M. Thiel. 1995. Modeling Reactive Behaviour in Vertically Layered Agent Architectures. In *ECAI-94: Proceedings of the Workshop on Agent Theories, Architectures, and Languages on Intelligent Agents*, ed. M. J. Wooldridge and N. R. Jennings, 261–276. New York: Springer.

Newell, A. and H. A. Simon. 1976. Computer Science as Empirical Enquiry. *Communication of the ACM* 19: 113–126.

Nwana, H. S. 1996. Software Agents: An Overview. *Knowledge Engineering Review* 11(3): 1–40.

Nwana, H. S., L. C. Lee, and N. R. Jennings. 1997. Coordination in Multi-Agent Systems. In *Software Agents and Soft Computing: Towards Enhancing Machine Intelligence*, Lecture Notes in Computer Science 1198, ed. H. S. Nwana and A. Nader, 42–58. Berlin: Springer.

Nwana, H. S. and D.T. Ndumu. 1998. A Brief Introduction to Software Agent Technology. In *Agent Technology: Foundations, Applications, and Markets*, ed. N. R. Jennings and M. J. Wooldridge, 29–47. New York: Springer.

O'Malley, S. A. and S. DeLoach. 2002. *Determining When to Use an Agent-Oriented Software Engineering Paradigm*. In AOSE '01: Revised Papers and Invited Contributions from the Second International Workshop on Agent-Oriented Software Engineering II, ed. M. J. Wooldridge, G. Weib, and P. Ciancarini, 188–205. Heidelberg: Springer Verlag.

OMG 2000. Mobile Agent Facility Specification V 1.0. Standard Document. www.omg.org/technology/documents/formal/mobile_agent_facility.htm (accessed January 5, 2009).

Omicini, A. 2001. SODA: Societies and Infrastructures in the Analysis and Design of Agent-Based Systems. In *Agent-Oriented Software Engineering*, ed. P. Ciancarini and M. J. Wooldridge, 185–193. Berlin: Springer.

Papadopoulos, G. A. 2001. Models and Technologies for the Coordination of Internet Agents: A Survey. In *Coordination of Internet Agents — Models, Technologies, and Applications*, ed. A. Omincini, F. Zambonelli, M. Klusch, and R. Tolksdorf, 25–56. Berlin: Springer.

Parunak, H. V. D. 1996. Applications of Distributed Artificial Intelligence in Industry. In Foundations of Distributed Artificial Intelligence, ed. G. M. P. O'Hare, and N. R. Jennings, 71–76. Chichester: John Wiley & Sons.

Petrie, C. 2001. Agent-Based Software Engineering. In *Agent-Oriented Software Engineering*, ed. P. Ciancarini and M. J. Wooldridge, 59–75. Berlin: Springer.

Pitt, J. and A. Mamdani. 2000. Communication Protocols in Multi-agent Systems: A Development Method and Reference Architecture. In *Issues in Agent Communication*. Lecture Notes in Computer Science 1916, ed. F. Dignum and M. Greaves, 160–177. Heidelberg: Springer.

Rao, A. S. and M. P. Georgeff. 1991. Modelling Rational Agents within a BDI-Architecture. In *Proceedings of the Second International Conference on Principles of Knowledge Representation and Reasoning*, ed. R. Fikes and E. Sandewall, 473–484. San Francisco, CA: Morgan Kaufman.

Rossi, D., G. Cabri, and E. Denti. 2001. Tuple-based Technologies for Coordination. In *Coordination of Internet Agents — Models, Technologies, and Applications*, ed. A. Omincini, F. Zambonelli, M. Klusch, and R. Tolksdorf, 83–109. Berlin: Springer.

Russell, S. J. and P. Norvig. 1995. *Artificial Intelligence A Modern Approach.* New Jersey: Prentice Hall.

Sadiig, I. A. M. J. 1997. An Autonomous Mobile Agent-Based Distributed Learning Architecture — A Proposal and Analytical Analysis. *The Turkish Online Journal of Distance Education* 6: 106–117.

Sánchez, J. A. 1997. A Taxonomy of Agents. Technical Report, Universidad de las Américas-Puebla, México.

Schoop, M. 2001. An Introduction to the Language-Action Perspective. *ACM SIGGROUP Bulletin* 11: 3–8.

Searle, J. R. 1969. *Speech Acts: An Essay in the Philosophy of Language.* Cambridge: Cambridge University Press.

Shannon, C. E. and W. Weaver. 1949. *The Mathematical Theory of Communication.* Champaign: University of Illinois Press.

Skarmeas, N. 1999. *Agent as Object with Knowledge Base State.* London: Imperial College Press.

Smolle, P. and Y. Sure. 2002 FRED: Ontology-Based Agents for Enabling E-Coaching Support in a Large Company. In *Proceedings of the 2nd International Workshop on Ontologies in Agent Systems (OAS 2002)*, ed. S J. Russell and P. Norvig, 68–70. Berlin: Springer.

Stone, P. and M. M. Veloso. 2003. Multiagent Systems: A Survey from a Machine Learning Perspective. *Autonomous Robots* 8: 345–383.

Sycara, K., A. Pannu, M. Williamson, D. Zeng, and K. Decker. 1996. Distributed Intelligent Agents. *IEEE Expert: Intelligent Systems and Their Applications* 11: 36–46.

Tanenbaum, A. and M. van Steen. 2002. *Distributed Systems, Principles and Paradigms.* New Jersey: Prentice Hall.

Tessier, C., L. Chaudron, and H. J. Müller. 2001. *Conflicting Agents — Conflict Management in Multi-Agent Systems.* Boston: Kluwer Academic.

Tidhar, G., A. Rao, M. Ljungberg, D. Kinny, and E. Sonenberg. 1992. Skills and Capabilities in Real-Time Team Formation. Technical Report, Australian Artificial Intelligence Institute, Melbourne, Australia.

Vasudevan, V. 1998. Comparing Agent Communication Languages. Technical Report, Object Services and Consulting Inc. www.objs.com (accessed January 5, 2009).

Walton, D. N. and E. C. W. Krabbe. 1995. *Commitment in Dialogue: Basic Concepts of Interpersonal Reasoning.* New York: State University of New York Press.

Wegner, P. 1996. Coordination as Constrained Interaction. In *Coordination Languages and Models — Proceedings of the First International Conference (COORDINATION'96)*, ed. P. Ciancarini and C. Hankin, 28–33. Los Altimos, CA: IEEE Computer Society Press.

Wille, C. 2005. Agent Measurement Framework. Ph.D. Thesis, University of Magdeburg, Shaker Publishing, Germany.

Wilsker, B. 1996. A Study of Multi-Agent Collaboration Theories. Technical Report, University of Southern California, Los Angeles.

Winograd, T. and F. Flores. 1986. *Understanding Computers and Cognition: A New Foundation for Design.* Norwood, NJ: Ablex Publishing.

Wong, H. C. and K. Sycara. 2000. A Taxonomy of Middle-Agents for the Internet. In *Proceedings of the 4th International Conference on Multi-Agent Systems (ICMAS-2000)*, 465–466. Los Altimos: IEEE Computer Society Press.

Wooldridge, M. J. and N. R. Jennings. 1995. Agent Theories, Architectures, and Languages: A Survey. In *Intelligent Agents: Theories, Architectures, and Languages*, ed. M. J. Wooldridge, and N. R. Jennings, 1–39. New York: Springer.

Wooldridge, M. J. and N. R. Jennings. 1995a. Intelligent Agents: Theory and Practice. *Knowledge Engineering Review* 10: 115–152.

Wooldridge, M. J. 1997. Agents as a Rorschach Test: A Response to Franklin and Graesser. In *Intelligent Agents III, Agent Theories, Architectures, and Languages, ECAI '96 Workshop (ATAL)*, ed. J. P. Müller, M. Wooldridge, and N. R. Jennings, 47–48.

Wooldridge, M. J. 2002. *An Introduction to Multi-Agent Systems.* Chichester: John Wiley & Sons.

2 Software Quality Assurance

2.1 QUALITY ASSURANCE BASICS

Basically, the general background on software quality assurance as software engineering itself is formulated. The following definition is the classical Institute of Electrical and Electronics Engineers' (IEEE) description of software engineering (Marciniak 1994, p. 1177): "Software engineering is the application of a systematic, disciplined, quantifiable approach to the development, operation, and maintenance of software; that is, the application of engineering to software."

This definition leads us to the simple visualization of software engineering components in Figure 2.1 (Dumke 2003; Marciniak 1994; Pfleeger 1998).

Considering this characterization, the following components of software engineering as basics for software quality assurance can be identified:

- *Software Engineering Methods*: "Structured approaches to software development, which include system models, notations, rules, design advice and process guidance" (Sommerville 2007, p. 11).
- *CASE (Computer-Aided Software Engineering)*: "Software systems which are intended to provide automated support for software process activities" (Sommerville 2007, p. 12).
- *A System of Measures*: A set of metrics and measures with which to measure and evaluate all aspects, components, and methodologies of the software engineering areas (Zuse 1998).
- *Software Engineering Standards*: The software engineering standards are a set of rules and principles as a foundation of control and examination of components achieving specially defined characteristics certified by a consortium like IEEE or International Standards Organization (ISO; Dumke 2003).
- *Software Systems*: A software system or a software product, respectively, "is a purposeful collection of interrelated components that work together to achieve some objectives" and requirements. It includes computer programs and the associated documentation (Sommerville 2007, p. 21).
- *Software Engineering Experience*: Experience summarizes the general aspects of laws, principles, criterions, methodologies, and theories in software engineering in the different forms of aggregation, correlation, interpretation, and conclusion based on a context-dependent interpretation (derived from Davis 1995).

- *Software Engineering Communities*: The software engineering community involves peoples, organizations, events, and initiatives in which interpersonal relationships make an integral part considering aspects or paradigms in software engineering (Figallo 1998).

Software development can be divided into three components: software product, software processes, and software resources, respectively. A *software product* can be described on the three components: model/architecture, implementation, and documentation, considering some of its quality characteristics (see Figure 2.2).

Quality aspects of *software processes* are based on the process areas: development phases or steps, management characteristics, and methodologies (see Figure 2.3).

Furthermore, quality assurance of *software resources* is based on the three resource components: personnel, software, and hardware (see Figure 2.4).

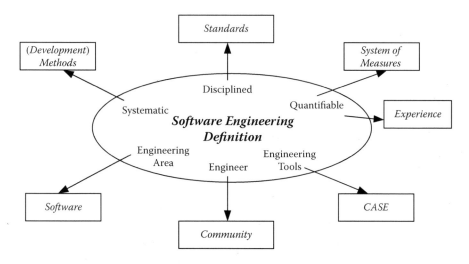

FIGURE 2.1   Basic characteristics of software engineering.

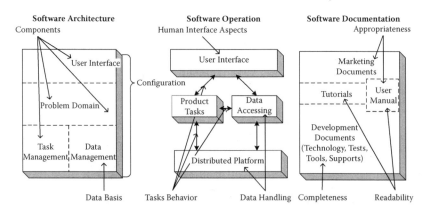

FIGURE 2.2   Simplified visualization of product evaluation aspects.

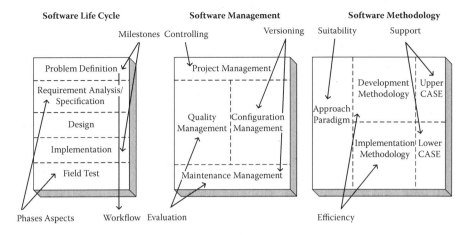

FIGURE 2.3 Simplified visualization of process quality aspects.

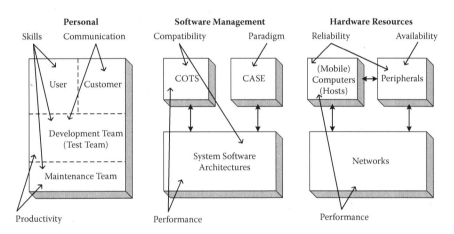

FIGURE 2.4 Simplified visualization of the resource's quality aspects.

Note that the described quality aspects are reasons, basics, and fundamentals of software quality. "A commonly mentioned measure of software quality is customer satisfaction" (Emam 2005, p. 14). *Quality assurance* includes the strategies, methodologies, tools, and (best) practices in order to achieve this goal.

Therefore, it is necessary to consider the main ingredients, aspects, and characteristics of software product, processes, and resources.

2.1.1 QUALITY ASSURANCE OF SOFTWARE SYSTEMS

Software systems and software products, respectively, should fulfill customer requirements. Based on essential experiences, the typical generally accepted quality aspects are summarized in the ISO 9126 standard (ISO/IEC 9126 2001). Table 2.1 shows these main quality aspects.

TABLE 2.1
ISO 9126 Quality Aspects

ISO 9126 Software System Quality Characteristic

Functionality	Suitability
	Accuracy
	Interoperability
	Compliance
	Security
Reliability	Maturity
	Fault tolerance
Usability	Understandability
	Learnability
	Operability
Efficiency	Time behavior
	Resource behavior
Maintainability	Analyzability
	Changeability
	Stability
	Testability
Portability	Adaptability
	Installability
	Conformance
	Replaceability

Missing quality can simply be identified by errors, failures, or defects. An overview about the essential indicators used to characterize defects is given in Emam (2005) as follows:

- *Defects and usage*: Usage is a function of the number of end users using the product, the number of actual machines executing the product, and the time since release.
- *Raw defect counts*: Defect density = (number of defects found)/size.
- *Adjusted defect density*: For example, adjusted by comparisons to "standard company."
- *Defect classification:* As defect priorities, defect severities, classification by problem type.

An overview about the delivered defects per function points (FPs), as a kind of software size, is shown in Table 2.2 (Emam 2005). Note that the FP-based software size of different products could be assumed as <100 FP for a small project, 100 FP ≤ medium project < 5000 FP, and >5000 FP for large projects (Jones 2007).

Quality assurance of software systems is based on constructive methods that prevent some classes of errors or defects. Constructive quality assurance methods are structured programming, code generation, and formal verification.

TABLE 2.2
Percentage of Respondents in a European Survey of Management Practices

Business Domain	Small Projects		Medium Projects		Large Projects	
	Average	Best	Average	Best	Average	Best
MIS (management information system)	0.15	0.025	0.588	0.066	1.062	0.27
System software	0.25	0.013	0.44	0.08	0.726	0.15
Commercial	0.25	0.013	0.495	0.08	0.792	0.208
Military	0.263	0.013	0.518	0.04	0.816	0.175

On the other hand, quality assurance can be based on analytical methods. Examples of this kind of quality assurance are software measurement and evaluation, statistical software processes, and software system visualization.

2.1.2 Quality Improvement of Software System Development

Examples of improvement standards and approaches for software development and software processes, respectively, are summarized as follows (described in Emam, Drouin, and Melo 1998; Garcia 2005; Royce 2005; Wang and King 2000).

- *ISO 9001:2000* is a standard for process assessment and certification comparable to other business areas and industries.
- *TickIT* informs the developer about actual quality issues and best practices considering the process improvement.
- *ISO 12207* defines the software life cycle processes for a general point of view and involves the process quality implicitly.
- *ISO 15504* is also known as SPICE (Software Process Improvement and Capability Determination).
- *Bootstrap* process evaluation is based on the assessment process, the process model (including the evaluation as *incomplete, performed, managed, established, predictable,* and *optimizing*), the questionnaires and the scoring, rating, and result presentation.
- *SEI-CMMI* is the well-known capability maturity model that *integrates* some of the other process improvement standards and approaches.
- *Trillium* is a Canadian initiative for software process improvement and provides the initiation and guidance of a continuous improvement program.
- *EFQM* (European Foundation of Quality Management) considers soft factors like customer satisfaction, policy and strategy, business results, motivation, and leading in order to evaluate the effectiveness and success of the process.

SPICE defines different *capability levels,* such as incomplete, performed, managed, established, predictable, and optimizing. The principles of the process

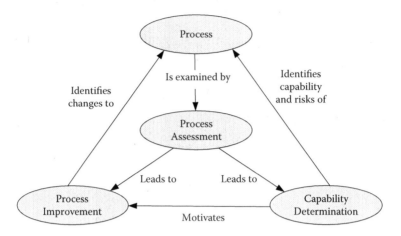

FIGURE 2.5   The SPICE (Software Process Improvement and Capability Determination) process assessment model.

assessment of SPICE are given in the semantic network (SPICE 2006) presented in Figure 2.5.

The special types of *process improvement phases* in the Six Sigma approach include and use five phases composing what is referred to as the *DMAIC* model (Tayntor 2003):

1. *Define* the problem and identify what is important (define the problem, form a team, establish a project charter, develop a project plan, identify customers, identify key outputs, identify and prioritize customer requirements, document the current process).
2. *Measure* the current process (determine what to measure, conduct the measurements, calculate the current sigma level, determine process capability, benchmark the process leaders).
3. *Analyze* what is wrong and potential solutions (determine what causes the variation, brainstorm ideas for process improvements, determine which improvements would have the greatest impact in meeting customer requirements, develop a proposed process map, and assess the risk associated with the revised process).
4. *Improve* the process by implementing solutions (gain approval for the proposed changes, finalize the implementation plan, implement the approved changes).
5. *Control* the improved process by ensuring that the changes are sustained (establish key metrics, develop the control strategy, celebrate and communicate success, implement the control plan, measure and communicate improvements).

Kandt (2006) summarizes different software process quality drivers, as shown in Table 2.3.

TABLE 2.3
Software Quality Drivers

	Boehm's Ranking	Clark's Ranking	Neufelder's Ranking
1	Personnel/team	Product complexity	Domain knowledge
2	Product complexity	Analyst capability	Nonprogramming managers
3	Required reliability	Programmer capability	Use of unit testing tools
4	Timing constraint	Constraint on execution time	Use of supported operating systems
5	Application experience	Personnel continuity	Testing of user documentation
6	Storage constraint	Required reliability	Use of automated tools
7	Modern programming practice	Documentation	Testing during each phase
8	Software tools	Multisite development	Reviewed requirements
9	Virtual machine volatility	Application experience	Use of automated fracas
10	Virtual machine experience	Platform volatility	Use of simulation

Putnam and Meyers (2003) define the *Five Core Metrics* for software process analysis, improvement, and controlling in the following manner:

1. *Quantity* of function, usually measured in terms of *size* (such as source lines of code or function points), that ultimately executes on the computer.
2. *Productivity,* as expressed in terms of the functionality produced for the time and effort expended.
3. *Time*, the duration of the project in calendar months.
4. *Effort,* the amount of work expended in person-months.
5. *Reliability,* as expressed in terms of defect rate (or its reciprocal, mean time effort).

The relationships of these core metrics are described by Putnam and Myers as follows: "People, working at some level of productivity, produce a quantity of function or a work product at a level of reliability by the expenditure of effort over a time interval" (2003, p. 34).

Table 2.4 shows the distribution of software process activities for different types of projects (Emam 2005).

The process tasks of *defect estimation* in software systems are summarized by Kandt (2006) in the following manner:

$$D_1 = (l \times d) - D_d \qquad (2.1)$$

where D_1 stands for the number of remaining defects in a module, l is the number code lines, d is the typical number of defects per source line of code, and D_d is the number of detected defects.

TABLE 2.4

Percentages of Process Activities in Different Kinds of Projects

Process Activity	Project (%)		
	System	Commercial	Military
Design	21	16	19
Requirements definition	11	6	13
Project management	17	16	17
Documentation	10	16	13
Change management	14	8	15
Coding	27	39	23

A special kind of *size estimation* based on the Rayleigh formula is known as a *software equation* (see also Keyes 2003):

$$\text{System\_size} = \text{technology\_constant} \times \text{Total\_effort}^{1/3} \times \text{duration}^{2/3} \qquad (2.2)$$

where the *technology_constant* depends on the development methodology.

The *customer cost* of a software product was executed by Emam (2005) in the following manner:

$$\text{Customer Cost} = \text{Defect\_density} \times \text{KLOC} \times \qquad (2.3)$$
$$\text{Cost\_per\_defect} \times \text{Defects\_find\_by\_customer}$$

The *return on investment (ROI)* was executed by Emam (2005) as follows:

$$\text{ROI}_1 = (\text{Cost saved} - \text{Investment})/\text{Investment} \qquad (2.4)$$

$$\text{ROI}_2 = (\text{Cost saved} - \text{Investment})/\text{Original cost} \qquad (2.5)$$

$$\text{New cost} = \text{Original cost} \times (1 - \text{ROI}_2) \qquad (2.6)$$

$$\text{Schedule reduction (Original schedule} - \text{New schedule})/ \qquad (2.7)$$
$$\text{Original schedule [personal month]}$$

These examples show different aspects of software development or software process evaluation and improvement:

- Software processes are based on life cycle structures, development approaches, including methodologies, and types of process management.
- Process quality improvement must consider all the essential and typical characteristics, such as capabilities, (cost) drivers, defect distributions, achieving economics, and aspect relationships and reasoning.

- Software development evaluation and control should be based on systematic approaches and methodologies, such as measurement-based modeling, analysis, evaluation, and exploration, using widely used improvement standards and techniques.

2.1.3 QUALITY ASSURANCE OF SYSTEM DEVELOPMENT RESOURCES

The following examples show some methods and aspects for resources evaluation, improvement, and management. The *personal software process* (PSP) considers the quality of the information technology (IT) personnel through analysis, evaluation, and improvement of their activities (Humphrey 2000). Figure 2.6 shows the essential steps of the PSP.

Based on the *telemetry project* from Johnson et al. (2005), Ullwer (2006) defined and implemented a background measurement and repository in order to automate the PSP using the *Hackystat* technology for Open Office.

Corbin's methodology for establishing a software development environment (SDE) includes the following procedures and issues (see Keyes 2003):

- *The Elements of SDE*: Project management, business plan, architecture, methodologies, techniques, tools, metrics, policies and procedures, technology platform, support, standards, education, and training.
- *The Benefits of SDE*: Improved problem definition; selection of the "right" problem according to the customer; joint customer and information system (IS) responsibilities and accountability; acknowledgement of customer

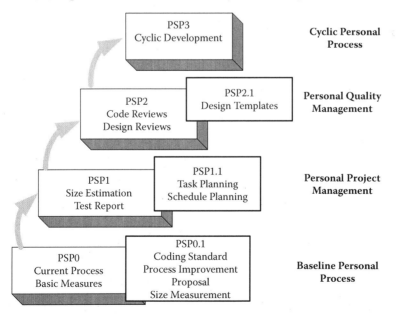

FIGURE 2.6   The personal software process (PSP) approach.

ownership of the system; reduced costs of system development and maintenance; reusability of software, models, and data definitions; acceptance of
the disciplined approach to software engineering using a consistent methodology; productivity improvements through team efforts and tools such
as CASE.
- *Sample Goals of SDE*: Reduce system development costs, reduce maintenance costs, reduce MIS turnover rate.

Essential knowledge about software components as COTS (commercial off-the-
shelf software), provided by Basili and Boehm (2001), includes:

1. More than 99% of all executing computer instructions come from COTS
   products. Each instruction passed a market test for value.
2. More than half of the features in large COTS software products go
   unused.
3. The average COTS software product undergoes a new release every 8 to 9
   months, with active vendor support for only its latest three releases.
4. Component-based software (CBS) development and postdeployment efforts
   can scale as high as the square of the number of independently developed
   COTS products targeted for integration.
5. CBS postdeployment costs exceed CBS development costs.
6. Although glue-code development usually accounts for less than half of the
   total CBS development effort, the effort per line of glue code averages about
   three times the effort per line of developed-application code.
7. Nondevelopment costs, such as licensing fees, are significant, and projects
   must plan for and optimize them.
8. CBS assessment and tailoring efforts vary significantly by COTS product
   classes — operating system, database management system, user interface,
   device driver, and so forth.
9. Personnel capability and experience remain the dominant factors influenc-
   ing CBS development productivity.
10. CBS is currently a high-risk activity, with effort and schedule overruns
    exceeding non-CBS software overruns. Yet many systems have used COTS
    successfully for cost reduction and early delivery.

Special methods and formulas for measuring *hardware reliability* based on failure rates and probabilistic characteristics of software systems include the following
(Singpurwalla and Wilson 1999):

- *Jelinski–Moranda Model*: Jelinski and Moranda assume that the software
  contains an unknown number of, say, N bugs and that each time the software fails, a bug is detected and corrected, and the failure rate T_i is propor-
  tional to $N - i + 1$, the number of remaining bugs in the code.
- *Baysian Reliability Growth Model*: This model is devoid of consideration
  that the relationship between the number of bugs and the frequency of failure is tenuous.

- *Musa–Okumoto Models*: These models are based on the postulation of a relationship between the intensity function and the mean value function of a Poisson process that has gained popularity with users.
- *General Order Statistics Model*: This kind of model is based on statistical order functions. The motivation for ordering comes from many applications, like hydrology, strength of materials, and reliability.
- *Concatenated Failure Rate Models*: These models introduce the infinite memories for storing the failure rates where the notion of infinite memory is akin to the notion of invertibility in time series analysis.

Quality assurance for software development resources involves the following aspects and characteristics:

- We must consider the personnel resources carefully because of their essential impact on software development, including the quality of the produced software system.
- Software resources are divided into used software, such as COTS, and software development tools, such as CASE tools. Quality assurance or evaluation of these types of resources involves the evaluation of the software processes of (external) tool vendors.
- Quality assurance of hardware/system resources is mainly based on analysis and (performance) evaluation of infrastructures integrated in existing hardware components using widespread system software (operating systems, networks, and collaboration systems).

2.2 QUALITY MEASUREMENT AND EVALUATION

Software measurement, including quality measurement, is one of the key processes in evaluating the quality of software products, processes, and involved resources. Usually the software measurement process is embedded in software engineering processes and depends on environmental characteristics such as the following (Abran et al. 2004; Ebert and Dumke 2007):

- The *estimation* of the next or future product components, process aspects, and resource levels for executing a successful continuous project in software development.
- The *analysis* of artifacts, technologies, and methods in order to understand the appropriate resources for the software process.
- The *structuring* of the software process for planning the next steps, including the resource characteristics.
- The *improvement* of techniques and methodologies for software development as software process improvement.
- The *control* of the software process, including the analysis of the product quality aspects and their relationships.

Such software measurement requires planning like any other project activity. That is one of the reasons that conceptual and software measurement framework approaches are necessary to realize software quality aspects and levels. The appropriateness of these measurement frameworks depends on their intentions and methodologies. Therefore, a brief general survey of the essential characteristics of software measurement, including aspects of the measurement processes, is provided.

2.2.1 Basics in Software Measurement

Software "measurement is the process by which numbers or symbols are assigned to attributes of entities in the real world in such a way as to describe them according to clearly defined rules" (Fenton and Pfleeger 1997, p. 28). In general, software measurement is motivated by measurement goals that were applied to measurement artifacts using measurement methods and leading to measurement results as numbers based on metrics or measures.

The different measurement goals can briefly be described as follows (Humphrey 2000; Kandt 2006; Munson 2003; Pandian 2004; Singpurwalla and Wilson 1999):

- The measurement goal of *understanding* considers essential knowledge about the measured artifacts of products, processes, and resources and is related mainly to the software user.
- The goal of *comprehension* describes the effort to understand some characteristics of the software artifacts by the developer.
- In our context, *learning* is the extension of the software engineering knowledge based on different measurement or experimentation methods related to personnel resources or communities.
- The measurement goal of *proving* considers the confirmation of any assumptions or hypotheses about the measured artifacts.
- The *validation* of software measurement is the process of ensuring that the measurement is a proper numerical characterization of the claimed attribute; this means showing that the representation condition is satisfied.
- The *improvement* is based on the artifacts' evaluation and describes the improved characteristics of these artifacts. The improvement could be one-dimensional or multidimensional. Note that the improvement is valid only for the considered aspect or attribute of a measurement object.
- The goal of *investigation* leads to the analysis of the given artifacts in the direction of assumed laws, rules, and hypotheses.
- The *exploration* considers the artifacts under a special point of view in order to recognize some meaningful new measurement goals and interesting artifacts.
- The *management* involves the activities of planning, assigning, coordinating, assessing, and correcting the software processes, including the appropriate resources.
- The *controlling* considers the interactions of components that will provide a desired component or system response as time progresses.
- The measurement goal of *certification* considers evaluation of the artifact by a special institutional community and by standardized assessment rules.

The measurement artifacts are given as software systems, software development processes, and involved resources. Figure 2.7 shows different levels of software measurement.

Software measurement can be performed directly (such as performance measurement) or can be model based (using graphs or artifact transformations). Using the measurement theory or statistical methods leads us to a measurement evaluation that is based on the measurement goals (see above). Figure 2.8 shows some different

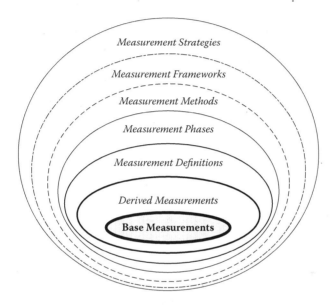

FIGURE 2.7 General aspects of software measurement.

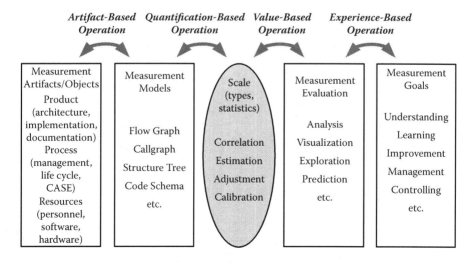

FIGURE 2.8 Software measurement of operations.

aspects in the context of model-based software measurement and evaluation achieving the intended goals.

In the following, special measurement and evaluation operations, describing some of the various kinds and details will be discussed.

2.2.2 MEASUREMENT METHODS AND PROCESSES

We briefly describe the relationship between measurement phases and measurement methods as characterized in Figure 2.9.

First, the *measurement phases* in their general context as the main steps of quality determination will be explained (Ebert and Dumke 2007; Wohlin 2000; Zuse 1998):

- *Modeling* is the reflection of the properties of a theory and, thereby, of some reality of which that theory is an abstract description.
- *Software measurement* is a technique or method that applies software measures to a (class of) software engineering object(s) to achieve a predefined goal.
- *Measurement analysis* is the process of integrating measures, decision criteria, and project context information to evaluate a defined information need.
- The purpose of *evaluation* is to provide an interested party with quantitative results concerning a software artifact that are comprehensible, acceptable, and trustworthy.
- The *measurement application* includes the different types of presentation, distribution, operation, and reaction.

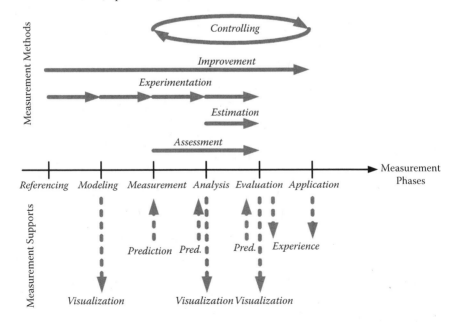

FIGURE 2.9   Software measurement of phases and methods.

The *measurement methods and supports* could be explained in a brief manner as follows:

- The *assessment* can be involved in all kinds of measurement, but the results are defined at a special point in time or moment.
- "*Estimation* is a process that uses prediction system and intuition for cost and resource planning. . . . It is concerned about assumptions regarding the future and the relevance of history" (Pandian 2004, p. 173).
- *Experimentation* is one of the empirical strategies for analysis and investigation, especially the controlled experiment.
- *Visualization* is a process of data analysis using graphical, optical, and other kinds of viewing techniques.
- "A *prediction system* consists of a mathematical model together with a set of prediction procedures for determining unknown variables and parameters" (Zuse 1998, p. 102).
- *Improvement* is based on evaluation of the artifacts and describes the kind of improved aspects and characteristics of these artifacts.
- *Controlling* considers the interactions of components that will provide a desired component or system response as time progresses.

Measurement analysis is "the process of integrating measures, decision criteria, and project context information to evaluate a defined information need" (McGarry et al. 2002, p. 39). Detailed methods of measurement analysis are as follows:

- The *transformation* includes all operations about the numbers produced by the measurement achieving special measurement goals and intentions.
- The "*regression analysis* is the process of determining how a variable, y, is related to one or more other variables, $x_1, x_2, \ldots, x_n$. The y variable is usually called the *response* by statisticians; the x_i's are usually called the *regressor* or simply the *explanatory variables*" (Berthold and Hand 2003, p. 70).
- The *factor analysis* considers the reduction of a large number of response variables to a smaller set of uncorrelated variables and interpretation of these newly created variables (Hanebutte, Taylor, and Dumke 2003).
- The *calibration* of measurement data is the modification of the numerical relational system without modifying the empirical relational system (Zuse 1998).
- The *unit transformation* is the modification of the measured value from one unit to another. It could be based on *conversion rules* describing the transformation of one measurement to another (Juristo and Moreno 2003).
- The *correlation* considers the relationship between different variables and is usually based on the correlation coefficient, which characterizes the dependency between the variables (Kitchenham et al. 1997).
- The *visualization* is a process of data analysis and has been explained above.
- The *adjustment* is the modification of the empirical relational system without modifying the numerical relational system based on (new) experience (Dumke et al. 1996).

- The *trend analysis* is a special kind of prediction considering a large future-directed time period and involving the artifacts (Kenett and Baker 1999).
- The *expertise* or *expert review* is a kind of evaluation of software artifacts involving the (defined) experts (Boehm et al. 2000).
- The *interpretation* includes extrapolation of the results from a particular sample to other environments, and it should be visible in professional forums for feedbacks. This activity is one of the sources for *experience building* for the different types of IT knowledge.

An essential aspect in measurement analysis is in the form of *metrics* (simple numbers or numbers with appropriate thresholds) or *measures* (including a measurement unit). For different sets of *measurement units,* some examples are described:

- Examples of *physical measure* units are Fahrenheit, gallon, gram, hertz, horsepower, hour, joule, karat, lux, meter, mile, millisecond, parsec, pound, watt, and yard.
- Examples of *economical measure units* are Euro, GNP (gross national product), hurdle rate, MBI (manpower buildup index), ROI (return on investment), $, share index, uninflated cost, and VAT (value added tax).
- Examples of *sociological measure units* are IQ (intelligence quotient), Mfactor (ordinal scaled part of motivation), StroudNumber, and Ufactor (part of unbroken working hours per day).
- Examples of *hardware measure units* are MTFD (mean time between failure and disclosure), MTDD (mean time between disclosure and diagnosis), MTDR (mean time between diagnosis and repair), MTFR (mean time between failure and repair), MTBF (mean time between failures), MTTD (mean time to defect), and MTTF (mean time to failure).
- Examples of *software measure units* are FP (function point), FP$^{(COSMIC)}$ (full function point by the COSMIC community), KDSI (kilo delivered source instruction), time$_{operation}$, PM (personnel [effort in] month), RSI (reused source instruction), and SLOC (source lines of code).

The measurement unit plays an important role in the operations of calibration, adjustment, and unit transformation or conversion.

Examples of *measurement evaluation* are heuristic evaluation, prospective evaluation, empirical evaluation, round-robin evaluation, snowball evaluation, and educational evaluation (Kitchenham, Pfleeger, and Fenton 1995).

Considering *measurement application,* the presentation and distribution extend the existing experiences in the software engineering area. Especially applications such as *operation* or *reaction* represent a form of *online measurement* (Pandian 2004).

The *measurement experience* summarizes the general aspects of the concrete measurement and results in different forms of aggregation, correlation, interpretation, and conclusion based on a context-dependent interpretation. Note that the measurement experience is divided into the experiences of the measurement results and the (evaluation-based) experience of the measurement. In the following, only the first aspect is considered. Some kinds of measurement experience are analogies, axioms, correlations, criterions, intuitions, laws, lemmas, formulas, methodologies, principles, relations, rules of thumb, and theories (Davis 1995; Endres and Rombach 2003; Kenett and Baker 1999).

The *measurement tools* are also called *computer-assisted measurement and evaluation* (CAME) tools (Dumke et al. 1996). Some typical kinds of CAME tools are summarized as follows: modeling tool, measurement tool, (statistical) analysis tool, visualization tool, and measurement repository tool.

Finally, the *principles of metrics application* are defined by Zuse (2003) as follows:

1. There is no best measure.
2. One number cannot express software quality.
3. The properties of the used measure should be well known.
4. One measure is not sufficient, because software systems consist of many properties.
5. A software quality or maintainability index, combined by many measures, has to be considered carefully.
6. It is a widespread misunderstanding that only the validated measures are useful.
7. It is important to know whether a measure assumes an extensive structure or not.
8. A measure that is validated in one environment is not automatically a validated measure.
9. A measure that has a good correlation to a validated measure is not automatically validated either.
10. The environment in every company for measurement is different.
11. There does not exist an initial set of measures or even a final set of measures.

2.3   SOFTWARE QUALITY ASSURANCE OF AGENT-BASED SYSTEMS

In the following, the quality measurement and evaluation of software agents, agent-based systems, and multiagent system (MAS) development will be discussed. Therefore, quality assurance will be described for each of these three agent-related areas. Furthermore, a set of potential metrics or measures for the product (agents and agent-based systems) and processes including the resources (MAS development) in order to fulfill the quality requirements are characterized.

The choice of appropriate measures depends upon the goals of the quality measurement — analyzing, evaluating, improving, or controlling. These measurement goals are founded in the empirical characteristics of an agent-based system based on the definition by Ferber (1999) or Dumke, Koeppe, and Wille (2000):

- The *quality* of the capability of acting in an environment.
- The *level* of communication with other agents.
- The *quantities* of the driven aspects by a set of tendencies.
- The *characteristics* of possessed resources.
- The *kind of capability* of perceiving its environment.

- The *characteristics* of the agent-based partial representation of this environment.
- The *quality* of the possessed skills and offered services.
- The *level* of the ability to reproduce itself.
- The *kind of behavior* toward satisfying its objectives, taking into account its resources.

2.3.1 GENERAL QUALITY ASPECTS OF SOFTWARE AGENTS

Chosen empirical aspects of *agent cooperation* could be characterized following Dumke, Koeppe, and Wille (2000):

- The *coordination of actions*, which concerns the adjustment of the direction of agents' actions in time and space.
- The *degree of parallelism*, which depends on the distribution of tasks and their concurrent execution.
- The *sharing of resources*, which concerns the use of resources and skills.
- The *robustness* of the system, which concerns the system's aptitude for making up for any failure by an agent.
- The *nonredundancy of actions*, which characterizes the low rate of redundant activities.
- The *nonpersistence of conflicts*, which testifies to the small number of blocking situations.

Some of the empirical characteristics of *the action and the behavior of software agents* could be described as follows (Huhns 2001; Wooldridge and Ciancarini 2001):

- The action characteristics of performance, complexity, and quality based on the different types of agent actions (transformation, influences, processes, modifications, displacement, and command).
- The *general types* of agents with or without memory and knowledge (*tropistic agents* and *hysteretic agents*).

Special aspects of the empirical characteristics of the *agent minds* are as follows (Ferber 1999; Vidahl, Buhler, and Huhns 2001):

- The structure and the complexity of the current MAS (interactional, representational, and conative).
- The *intensity* of the *motivation* of the different kinds of software agents.
- The *appropriateness* of the *commitments* of agents related to the general system intention.
- The *relationship* of the software agent intention to each other.

Finally, some of the empirical aspects of *agent coordination and collaboration* can be described as follows (Jennings and Wooldridge 1998; Knapik and Johnson 1998; Papadopoulos 2001):

- The *level* and *intensity* of communication between software agents.
- The *kind* and the *quality* of coordination between interacting agents.
- The *intention* of collaboration as the basis of the evaluation of agent efficiency.
- The *volume* and the *efficiency* of the cooperation.
- The *increasing of the agent facilities* and knowledge during the collaboration.

Considering the empirical aspects above, the following metrics set for the measurement and evaluation of software agents are defined (Dumke, Koeppe, and Wille 2000; Wille, Dumke, and Stojanov 2002, 2002a):

The metrics for the *agent design level* are as follows:

- *Software agent size*: The size considers both aspects of an agent: the functional size and the physical size of a software agent. A large agent size can cause low performance and mobility.
- *Software agent component structure*: The structure depends upon the kind of the agent (intelligent, reactive, deliberative, etc.), and the agent interface is related to the kind of agent coupling (as fixed, variable, or evolutionary). The structure affects the changeability.
- *Software agent complexity*: The complexity is divided into computational and psychological complexity and should be measured using concrete aspects. A high computational complexity leads to weak performance.
- *Software agent functionality*: This aspect considers the appropriateness of the agent with respect to the requirements. A high functionality can inhibit the chosen object-oriented implementation paradigm.

The metrics for the *agent description level* include:

- *Software agent development description level*: It considers the completeness of the development documentation (including tests and change supports). The description level determines the maintainability of an agent.
- *Software agent application description level*: The metric includes the quality (readability, completeness, online support, etc.) of the user documentation. This evaluation considers the usability of a software agent.
- *Software agent publication description level*: This metric considers the public relations for using the software agent and involves the system description. A high publication level supports spreading the agent use.

The metrics for the *agent working level* include:

- *Software agent communication level*: Considers the size of communication and the level of conversation required to sustain the activities. High communication intensity can affect a flexible application.
- *Software agent interaction level*: This metric is related to the agent's context and environment and an agent's different kinds of actions (as transformation, reflecting, executing, modification, commands, perception, and deliberation). This aspect expresses the activity of an agent.

- *Software agent learning level*: This metric evaluates the skills, intentions, and actions of extending the agent facilities. This level is based on the agent's type and its roles within the system.
- *Software agent adaptation level*: The adaptation metric considers facilities of an agent, changing in order to react to new conditions in the environment. The facility of adaptation determines the stability of the agent implementation.
- *Software agent negotiation level*: This measure is based on the evaluation of facilities like the agent intentions, conflict resolution, and realized commitments for successful negotiation. This level determines the success of an agent activity relating to common tasks.
- *Software agent collaboration level*: This metric is oriented toward the agent's facility to work together with other agents. The collaboration of an agent classifies its roles in the given tasks.
- *Software agent coordination level*: The agent's facility of managing any one agent task is considered. This level determines the role of the agent in an administration hierarchy.
- *Software agent cooperation level*: This metric considers the volume and efficiency of an agent relating to a common task. This level determines the effectiveness of common task realization.
- *Software agent self-reproduction level*: The number of destroyed agents related to repaired agents is counted. This level determines the stability of a software agent.
- *Software agent performance level*: This metric considers the task-related performance of an agent. A high-level agent performance is related to all kinds of agent activities.
- *Software agent specialization level*: This metric considers the degree of specialization and the degree of redundancy of an agent. High specialization can lead to high performance.

2.3.2 GENERAL QUALITY ASPECTS OF MULTIAGENT SYSTEMS (MASS)

Typical quality measurement goals for MASs are founded in the empirical characteristics of MASs based on the definition by Ferber (Ferber 1999) and Dumke, Koeppe, and Wille (2000):

- The *volume* and *structure* of an agent environment E.
- The position in E of the objects, O, which are active. Passive objects have the status of perceived, created, or destroyed.
- The level of assembly of agents, A, that are specific objects, representing the active entities of the system.
- The intensity of the relations, R, which link objects (and thus agents) to each other.
- The performance of the operations, Op, making it possible for the agents of A to perceive, produce, consume, transform, and manipulate objects from O.

- The *complexity* of the operators with the task of representing the application of these operations and the reaction of the world to this attempt at modifications, which will be called the laws of the universe.

With respect to *agent organizations,* the following empirical aspects can be established (Ferber 1999; Omicini 2001; Shehory 2001):

- The characteristics of the agents' functions in the organization (representational, organizational, conative, interaction, operative, and preservative).
- The *quality aspects* of analysis dimensions of software agents (*physical, social, relational, environmental,* and *personal*) in the organization.
- The *complexity* of the agents' coupling (*fixed, variable,* and *evolutionary*).
- The *effectiveness* of the agent's organization with respect to its *redundancy* and *specialization.*

With respect to the empirical aspects above, the following metric or measure sets for the quality measurement and evaluation of MASs are defined (Dumke, Koeppe, and Wille 2000; Wille, Dumke, and Stojanov 2002, 2002a).

The metrics for the *MAS design level* are as follows:

- *Agent system size*: The measured system size includes the potential number of (active) agents and their contents; further, the size is related to the environment. A small agent system size can reduce the application area.
- *Agent system component structure*: This metric includes agent's type of organizational structure (hierarchies or egalitarian), the degree of parallelism, and the type of organizational functions (representational, organizational, conative, interactional, productive, or preservative). The system structure relates to the performance and the system changeability.
- *Agent system complexity*: One of these measured aspects leads to the degree of the organizational dimensions (social, relational, physical, environmental, and personal). This aspect influences the system applicability.
- *Agent system functionality*: This metric considers the realization of all functional system requirements. The distribution of the functionality in the system components influences their flexibility.

The metrics for the *MAS description level* are as follows:

- *Agent system development description level*: This metric considers the integration of the agent concepts and dynamics and their sufficient documentation. This system description affects system maintenance.
- *Agent system application description level*: This considers the user documentation of all aspects of the system applications related to the different user categories. A good application description is a precondition for efficient use of the whole system.
- *Agent system publication description level*: Publication metrics evaluate the user acceptance and marketing aspects of the agent-based system

application. A good system publication supports the spread of the system, especially within the educational area.

The metrics for the *MAS working level* are as follows:

- *Agent system communication level*: The number of agent communication languages (ACLs) between the different kinds of software agents and their different roles and actions. This level characterizes the intensity of the conversations and describes the agent collaboration.
- *Agent system interaction level*: This metric deals with the average types of interactions relating to the agents and their roles in the environment of the agent-based system. Many interactions are based on high cooperation levels.
- *Agent system knowledge level*: This metric measures the results of agent learning for an agent-based system (based on the different kinds of agents, either tropistic or hysteretic). This aspect determines the knowledge-based foundation of the agent-based system.
- *Agent system lifeness level*: This metric is based on the agent adaptation that reflects the adaptation level of the whole agent-based system. This aspect is based on the adaptability of the agents and characterizes the system maintenance effort.
- *Agent system conflict management level*: The system success is based on agent negotiation and considers the relations between the different kinds of fair play in the realization of the system tasks. A high conflict management level leads to high system stability.
- *Agent system community level*: This metric considers the level of different agent communities based on the agent collaboration. A high community level is caused by the collaboration of different classes of system application.
- *Agent system management level*: This system metric is based on the agent coordination level with respect to the whole agent system structure. A high management level expresses a good agent organization level.
- *Agent system application level*: This metric is related to the application area and the different agent roles in cooperation. A high application level is reflected in effective task-oriented agent cooperation.
- *Agent system stability level*: The stability measure is based on agent self-reproduction. A high stability level includes agent self-reproduction and other system error handling facilities.
- *Agent system performance level*: Handling with the goal of realizing special tasks through different agents is considered. This level includes agent performance and performance of the environment.
- *Agent system organization level*: The different agent roles (archivist, customer, mediator, planner, decision maker, observer, and communicator). This level leads to an efficient distribution of the agent roles and their administration.

2.3.3 GENERAL QUALITY ASPECTS OF MAS DEVELOPMENT

The third quality measurement area to be addressed with respect to the MAS consists of the MAS development process, including the resources used (personnel, software, and hardware).

First, the MAS development process, including the aspects of the life cycle, the development methods, and the tasks of managing this process, which defines the following metrics and measures set is considered (Dumke, Koeppe, and Wille 2000; Wille, Brehmer, and Dumke 2004).

The metrics for the *agent development life cycle* are as follows:

- *Software agent phases level*: The characteristics (size, structure, complexity) in the different development phases are considered. A high phase level is expressed by a high level of verification.
- *Software agent milestones level*: This metric evaluates agent development with respect to a milestone. This level expresses the correct timing of the agent development.
- *Software agent requirements workflow level*: This metric considers the implemented requirements during the development phases. This level is caused by the timely realization of the requirements for agent implementation.

The metrics for the *agent development method level* are as follows:

- *Software agent methodology level*: The level of the development method used is quantified. This level means that the development method should be adequate for the type of agent implementation.
- *Software agent paradigm level*: This metric evaluates the appropriateness of the chosen development paradigm. A high paradigm level is caused by the appropriate choice for the implementation technique.
- *Software agent CASE level*: This metric quantifies the tool support for agent implementation. This level reflects tool support during agent development.

The following are the metrics for the *agent development management level*:

- *Agent project management level*: This set of metrics considers the management level of the development risks and methods. A high level of management is involved in the system project management.
- *Agent configuration management level*: This considers the success of the version control with respect to an agent. This level reflects the quality of version control for the software agent.
- *Agent quality management level*: This set of metrics considers the quality assurance techniques related to an agent. This level reflects the quality assurance techniques related to agent development.

Now, the development process of the MAS is considered and the following appropriate software metrics for the measurement and evaluation of these aspects is defined.

The following are the metrics for the *MAS development life cycle*:

- *Agent system phases level*: This evaluation considers the system metrics of size, structure, and complexity during system development. This level is caused by appropriate development results for an efficient system realization.
- *Agent system milestones level*: This metric evaluates MAS development with respect to a milestone. This level is related to all development aspects in the planning phase of their realization.
- *Agent system requirements workflow level*: The requirements implementation during the development phases in the whole system is considered. A high workflow level evaluates the appropriateness of the realized system requirements.

The metrics for the *MAS development method* are as follows:

- *Software MAS methodology level*: The level of the used development method is quantified. A high methodology level reflects the use of appropriate development techniques.
- *Software MAS paradigm level*: This metric evaluates the appropriateness of the chosen development paradigm. This level determines the appropriateness of the chosen techniques for system implementation.
- *Software MAS CASE level*: This metric quantifies the tool support for the agent implementation. This level includes the set of different tools needed to support system development.

The metrics for the *MAS development management level* are as follows:

- *System project management level*: The management level of the development risks and methods of the system is considered. This level describes the timing and the appropriate use of resources for system development.
- *System configuration management level*: This metric includes evaluation of the dynamic aspects of the system configuration. This level is affected by using version control for all parts of the agent-based system.
- *System quality management level*: The quality assurance techniques related to the whole agent-based system are considered. This level includes the different quality assurance techniques.

The agent and MAS development process require different resources, such as personnel (developer, tester, administrator, and so on), software resources (MAS COTS and CASE tools), and platform resources, including the hardware components. Therefore, measurement values with respect to the characteristics (especially the quality) of these resources is needed. Hence, the following metrics that are also necessary to evaluate the MAS development process are defined.

The metrics for the *agent developer level* include:

- *Agent developer skill level*: This metric is related to the skills to develop and implement a software agent. A high skill level expresses good developer specialization for agent implementation.
- *Agent developer communication level*: The ability of the developer to improve its work by collaboration and cooperation is considered. Communication is an indicator for the efficient resolution of any questions.
- *Agent developer productivity level*: This metric evaluates the quantity of work. High productivity includes functionality and the quality of the software agent.

The following are the metrics for the *agent software resources level*:

- *Agent software paradigm level*: This metric evaluates the appropriateness of the chosen software basis and used software components for the implementation of a software agent. This level reflects the appropriateness of the chosen paradigm.
- *Agent software performance level*: This metric addresses the software components and their effectiveness. This level is a precondition for agent performance and is related to the system software used.
- *Agent software replacement level*: This metric considers the effort of adaptation when using different versions of the basic software. A high replacement level reflects a large quantity of agent maintenance and migration.

The metrics for the agent hardware resources level are as follows:

- *Agent hardware reliability level*: This metric considers reliability of the types of hardware required for running the software agent. This level reflects the different platforms that will be used by a mobile agent.
- *Agent hardware performance level*: This set of metrics considers the platforms used for an agent. This level also considers the potential types of platforms.
- *Agent hardware availability level*: The average availability of the different platforms used from a (mobile) agent is considered. A high availability level is a precondition for the mobility of an agent.

The following are the metrics for the *MAS developer level*:

- *System developer skill level*: This metric is based on agent developer skills and is extended by the (dynamic) system characteristics. This level reflects the different kinds of knowledge used to develop the different components of the agent-based system.
- *System developer communication level*: This set of metrics considers the ability of the developer(s) to improve its work by collaboration and cooperation. A high communication level is based on the successful design techniques of the participants.

- *System developer productivity level*: The quantity of work is considered. This level is related to the development of the different system components.

The metrics for the *MAS software resources level* are as follows:

- *System software paradigm level*: The appropriateness of the chosen software basis and COTS system used for the implementation of the agent-based system is evaluated. This level is divided into the different system components.
- *System software performance level*: This metric considers the evaluation of the efficiency of the involved software base and the external components. The system performance of the COTS used indicates a high performance level.
- *System software replacement level*: The adaptation to the different versions of the basic software is considered. This level is divided into the evaluation of the different components of the agent-based system.

The metrics for the *MAS hardware resources level* are as follows:

- *System hardware reliability level*: The reliability of the kinds of hardware for running the agent-based system is considered. This level includes all platforms of the implemented environment of the agent-based system.
- *System hardware performance level*: This set of metrics considers the platforms used for an agent-based system. This level is a basis for the efficiency of the agent-based system.
- *System hardware availability level*: The average availability of the different platforms used with the agent-based system is considered. This level expresses the stability of the system used.

The given metrics and measure set for quality assurance of agent-based systems are meaningful and concluded by a holistic point of view of all the software engineering quality aspects. The following three chapters show the current state and situations of quality measurement of agent-based systems and development methodologies.

REFERENCES

Abran, A., M. Bundschuh, G. Büren, and R. R. Dumke. 2004. *Software Measurement — Research and Application*. Aachen, Germany: Shaker.

Berthold, M. and D. J. Hand. 2003. *Intelligent Data Analysis*. New York: Springer.

Basili, V. R. and B. W. Boehm. 2001. COTS-Based Systems Top 10 List. *IEEE Computer* 36: 91–95.

Boehm, B. W. et al. 2000. *Software Cost Estimation with COCOMO II*. New Jersey: Prentice Hall.

Davis, A. M. 1995. *201 Principles of Software Development*. New York: McGraw-Hill.

Dumke, R. 2003. *Software Engineering* (German). Wiesbaden: Vieweg.

Dumke, R., E. Foltin, R. Koeppe, and A. Winkler. 1996. *Software Quality Assurance with Measurement Tools* (German). Braunschweig, Germany: Vieweg.

Dumke, R., R. Koeppe, and C. Wille. 2000. Software Agent Measurement and Self-Measuring Agent-Based Systems, Preprint No. 11, Department of Computer Science, University of Magdeburg, Germany.

Ebert, C. and R. Dumke. 2007. *Software Measurement — Establish, Extract, Evaluate, Execute*. New York: Springer.

Eman, K. E. 2005. *The ROI from Software Quality*. Boca Raton, FL: Auerbach.

Emam, K. E., J. N. Drouin, and W. Melo. 1998. *SPICE — The Theory and Practice of Software Process Improvement and Capability Determination*. Los Altimos, CA: IEEE Computer Society Press.

Endres, A. and D. Rombach. 2003. *A Handbook of Software and Systems Engineering — Empirical Observation, Laws and Theories*. Reading, MA: Addison-Wesley.

Fenton, N. E. and S. L. Pfleeger. 1997. *Software Metrics — A Rigorous and Practical Approach*. London: Chapman & Hall.

Ferber, J. 1999. *Multi-Agent Systems — An Introduction to Distributed Artificial Intelligence*. Reading, MA: Addison-Wesley.

Figallo, C. 1998. *Hosting Web Communities*. Chichester: John Wiley & Sons.

Garcia, S. 2005. How Standards Enable Adoption of Project Management Practice. *IEEE Software* 22: 22–29.

Hanebutte, N., C. Taylor, and R. R. Dumke. 2003. Techniques of successful application of factor analysis in software measurement. *Empirical Software Engineering* 8(1): 43–57.

Huhns, M. N. 2001. Interaction-Oriented Programming. In *Agent-Oriented Software Engineering*. Lecture Notes in Computer Science 1957, ed. P. Ciancarini and M. J. Wooldridge, 29–44. New York: Springer.

Humphrey, W. S. 2000. The Personal Software Process: Status and Trends. *IEEE Software* 17: 71–75.

ISO/IEC9126 2001. Software Engineering-Product quality. Standard Document, Geneva, www.iso.org (accessed January 5, 2009).

Jennings, N. R. and M. J. Wooldridge. 1998. *Agent Technology — Foundation, Applications and Markets*. Berlin: Springer.

Johnson, P. M., H. Kou, M. Paulding, Q. Zhang, A. Kagaw, and T. Yamashita. 2005. Improving Software Development Management through Software Project Telemetry. *IEEE Software* 22: 78–85.

Jones, C. 2007. *Estimating Software Costs — Bringing Realism to Estimating*. New York: McGraw-Hill.

Juristo, N. and A. M. Moreno. 2003. *Basics of Software Engineering Experimentation*, Boston: Kluwer Academic.

Kandt, R. K. 2006. *Software Engineering Quality Practices*. Boca Raton, FL: Auerbach.

Kenett, R. S. and E. R. Baker. 1999. *Software Process Quality — Management and Control*. Los Angeles: Marcel Dekker.

Keyes, J. 2003. *Software Engineering Handbook*. Boca Raton, FL: Auerbach.

Kitchenham, B., S. L. Pfleeger and N. Fenton. 1995. Towards a Framework for Software Measurement Validation. *IEEE Transactions on Software Engineering* 21(12): 929-944.

Kitchenham, B., P. Brereton, D. Budgen, S. Linkman, V. L. Almstrum, and S. L. Pfleeger. 1997. Evaluation and Assessment in Software Engineering. *Information and Software Technology* 39(11): 731–734.

Knapik, M. and J. Johnson. 1998. *Developing Intelligent Agents for Distributed Systems*. New York: McGraw-Hill.

Marciniak, J. J. 1994. *Encyclopedia of Software Engineering*. Vol. I and II. Chichester: John Wiley & Sons.

McGarry, J., D. Card, C. Jones, B. Layman, E. Clark, J. Dean, and F. Hall. 2002. *Practical Software Measurement*. Reading, MA: Addison-Wesley.

Munson, J. C. 2003. *Software Engineering Measurement*. Boca Raton, FL: CRC Press.

Omicini, A. 2001. SODA: Societies and Infrastructures in the Analysis and Design of Agent-Based Systems. In *Agent-Oriented Software Engineering*, ed. P. Ciancarini and M. J. Wooldridge, 185–193. Berlin: Springer.

Pandian, C. R. 2004. *Software Metrics — A Guide to Planning, Analysis and Application.* Boca Raton, FL: CRC Press.

Papadopoulos, G. A. 2001. Models and Technologies for the Coordination of Internet Agents: A Survey. In *Coordination of Internet Agents — Models, Technologies, and Applications*, ed. A. Omincini, F. Zambonelli, M. Klusch, and R. Tolksdorf, 25–56. Berlin: Springer.

Pfleeger, S. L. 1998. *Software Engineering — Theory and Practice.* New Jersey: Prentice-Hall.

Putnam, L. H. and W. Myers. 2003. *Five Core Metrics — The Intelligence Behind Successful Software Management.* New York: Dorset House.

Royce, W. 2005. Successful Software Management Style: Steering and Balance. *IEEE Software* 22: 40–47.

Shehory, O. 2001. Software Architecture Attributes of Multi-Agent Systems. In *Agent-Oriented Software Engineering*, Lecture Notes in Computer Science 1957, ed. P. Ciancarini and M. J. Wooldridge, 77–90. Berlin: Springer.

Singpurwalla, N. D. and S. P. Wilson. 1999. *Statistical Methods in Software Engineering*, Berlin: Springer.

Sommerville, I. 2007. *Software Engineering.* Reading, MA: Addison-Wesley.

SPICE 2006. The SPICE Web Site. Community Documents. www.sqi.gu.edu.au/spice/ (accessed January 5, 2009).

Tayntor, C. B. 2003. *Six Sigma Software Development.* Boca Raton, FL: Auerbach.

Ullwer, C. 2006. Modelling and Prototypical Implementation of a Telemetric-Based Measurement Architecture (German). Diploma Thesis, Department of Computer Science, University of Magdeburg, Germany.

Vidahl, J. M., P. A. Buhler, and M. N. Huhns. 2001. Inside an Agent. *IEEE Internet Computing* 5: 82–86.

Wang, Y. and G. King. 2000. *Software Engineering Processes — Principles and Applications.* Boca Raton, FL: CRC Press.

Wille, C., N. Brehmer, and R. Dumke. 2004. Software Measurement of Agent-Based Systems — An Evaluation Study of the Agent Academy. Department of Computer Science, University of Magdeburg, Germany.

Wille, C., R. Dumke, and S. Stojanov. 2002. Quality Assurance in Agent-Based Systems Current State and Open Problems. Department of Computer Science, University of Magdeburg, Germany.

Wille, C., R. Dumke, and S. Stojanov. 2002a. New Measurement Intentions in Agent-Based Systems Development and Application. In *Software Measurement and Estimation*, Proceedings of the 12th International Workshop on Software Measurement, ed. R. Dumke et al., 203–227. Aachen: Shaker.

Wohlin, C. 2000. *Experimentation in Software Engineering: An Introduction*, Boston: Kluwer Academic.

Wooldridge, M. J. and P. Ciancarini. 2001. Agent-Oriented Software Engineering: State of the Art. In *Agent-Oriented Software Engineering*, Lecture Notes in Computer Science 1957, ed. P. Ciancarini, and M. J. Wooldridge, 1–28. Berlin: Springer.

Zuse, H. 1998. *A Framework of Software Measurement.* Berlin: De Gruyter.

Zuse, H. 2003. What Can Practitioners Learn from Measurement Theory. In *Investigations in Software Measurement*, ed. R. Dumke and A. Abran, 175–176. Aachen: Shaker.

3 Agent Quality Measurement and Evaluation

3.1 INTRODUCTION

Software agents can be applied to solve new types of problems as they may arise in *dynamic open systems* (Jennings and Wooldridge 1998), so the structure of the system is capable of changing dynamically, and as its components are not known in advance, they can change over time and may be highly heterogeneous. In order to manage software systems like this, some current types and methods of quality measurement and evaluation techniques will be considered. First, the essential components of a software agent from a measurement point of view will be shown in the scheme of Figure 3.1.

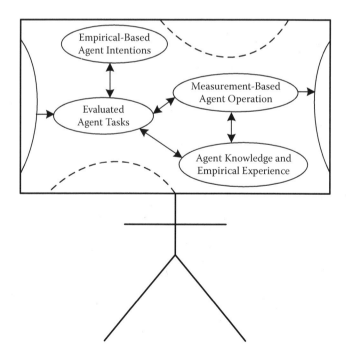

FIGURE 3.1 Measurement-based components of a general software agent.

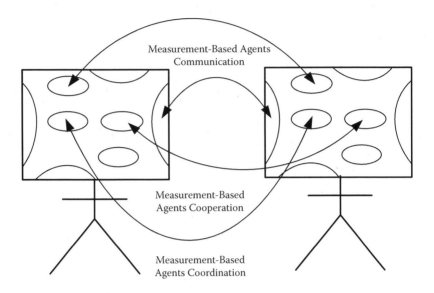

FIGURE 3.2   Measurement-based communication between software agents.

Other aspects of software agents are related to their communication or cooperation. Figure 3.2 explains these aspects in general (Dumke 2000; Wille, Dumke, and Stojanov 2002).

The general quality aspects of software agents are discussed in Chapter 2. Here, a description is provided of the existing approaches in order to determine the different characteristics of software agents achieving their quality assurance.

3.2   REVIEW OF AGENT MEASUREMENT EXAMPLES

3.2.1   Performance Measurement by Sycara

Performance measurement functions are integrated in the RETSINA toolkit so that the agents can be *self-aware,* which means that they can measure their own performance and optimize themselves (Sycara et al. 2003).

The *response time* (T_r) will vary with the latencies according to the following expression:

$$T_r = T_{not} + T_{del} + T_{cre} + T_{com} \tag{3.1}$$

There is an associated delay for the following:

- Time to notify (T_{not})
- Time to delete (T_{del})
- Time to create (T_{cre})
- Time to commit (T_{com})

In the area of an agent-based e-commerce recommendation system, Kim and Cho (2003) used the *response time* as a performance evaluation metric. Based on it, they present a performance comparison of different algorithms.

3.2.2 EXECUTION TIME BY GUICHARD AND AYEL

The execution time is used by Guichard and Ayel (1995) to evaluate the effectiveness of the self-organization of agents. The agents are prolog processes, and they have to solve the research of prime numbers. The agents are able to act introspectively to determine the needed time for verification of a number with its known prime numbers and to compare it to the required time.

3.2.3 PERFORMANCE SIMULATION BY PHAM

In Pham (2002), a simulation is used to estimate the performance of agent-based generic methods. The following two criteria were used:

1. Computation time Tc to evaluate the performance.
2. Response time Trp to evaluate the quality of service.

The simulation results show significant differences between the analyzed methods.

3.2.4 PERFORMANCE EVALUATION BY SUGAWARA ET AL.

An example for the usage of agents to fix the problem of the increasing amount of information in telecommunication networks is presented by Sugawara, Yamaoka, and Sakai (2001). They used a simulation to evaluate the performance of different algorithms for information search agents. A 100-node lattice network in a 10-by-10 pattern was given, and the search nodes were randomly selected from the nodes. They ran simulations for 10, 30, and 50 nodes and used the time costs for searching to evaluate the performance of the agent's search algorithms.

3.2.5 MONITORING AND RECORDING AGENT PERFORMANCE BY TAMBE

The Karma Teamcore framework is based on distributed, heterogeneous agents and the tasking of them via an abstract team-oriented program (Tambe, Pynadath, and Chauvat 2000). While the team executes a program, the framework allows monitoring and recording of the execution to provide feedback for the developer. The observations are nonintrusive and are based on eavesdropping on the multicast messages that the Teamcore wrappers send as part of their normal operation. Karma also records how well agents perform the current task. All information is maintained in the local database, and the developer can debug after a failure occurs.

3.2.6   Performance Measurement by Russel and Norvig

A general introduction to agent-related performance measurement is given in Russell and Norvig (2003). An agent plunking down in its environment generates a sequence of actions, and if the sequence is desirable, the agent performed well. "Obviously, there is not one fixed measure suitable for all agents" (Russell and Norvig 2003, p. 106). One way to get information about agent performance is to ask the agent how happy it is about its own performance. But this is a subjective opinion, and an objective performance measure should be imposed by the developer who was constructing the agent. Using an example with a vacuum cleaner agent, Russell describes four aspects that should be provided by any rational agent:

1. The performance measure that defines the criterion of success.
2. The agent's prior knowledge of the environment.
3. The action that the agent can perform.
4. The agent's percepts sequence to date.

In another example, Russell describes how to measure the problem-solving performance of an algorithm used by an agent. He proposes four ways to evaluate an algorithm's performance:

1. *Completeness* as the guarantee of the algorithm to find a solution.
2. *Optimality* as the strategy to find the optimal solution.
3. *Time complexity* as the time it takes to find the solution.
4. *Space complexity* as how much memory is needed to perform the search.

In a general manner as a test-bed environment for intelligent agents, they give the following performance measurement details: +1000 for picking up the gold, –1000 for falling into a pit or being eaten by the wumpus, –1 for each action taken, and –10 for using up the arrow.

3.2.7   Problem-Solving Performance by Joshi

A multiagent system (MAS) where problem-solver agents interact with their neighbors in pursuing autonomous goals is presented in Joshi, Ramakrishnan, and Houstis (1998). Based on C language and shell scripts, the Pythia agent system is presented. Using the Knowledge Query Manipulation Language (KQML), the agents can communicate with each other. Certain individual agents are experts in problem solving and can ask other agents for help. The first step in learning is to find out which other agent has the best strategy for solving the given problem. A special agent called Pythia-C is used as a master agent with the purpose to learn. To find the algorithm with the best performance, the time needed by different learning algorithms of a Pythia-C agent to solve the problem can be used. The results demonstrate that all used learning techniques are adequate in the sense that the Pythia-C agent could find the best agent for each problem class with greater than 90% accuracy. Tests have been performed with problems in larger and smaller training sets. After measuring the time for problem solving, Joshi explains that the neurofuzzy learning method performs best. The performance measure is broken down to the time that the agent needs to find the agent with the best problem-solving algorithm.

They analyze scenarios with static and dynamic changing environments, and they implement time-based, reactive, and time-based reactive schemes. Time-based means that the agent reverts to learning mode at periodic time steps. In the reactive scheme, the Pythia-C agent broadcasts information, when their confidence for some class of problems has changed significantly. The time-based reactive scheme is a combination of the first two approaches. A Pythia-C agent sends out a message at periodic intervals, asking if any agent's abilities have significantly changed, and switches to learning mode if it receives an affirmative reaction. In this approach, the time steps for training are used as a performance measure, to evaluate agent learning by comparing different problem-solving sets.

3.2.8 PERFORMANCE ANALYSIS OF MOBILE AGENTS BY KOTZ ET AL.

The performance analysis in wireless networks as an ideal environment for mobile agents is presented in Kotz et al. (2002). In an environment with low bandwidth and low reliability, Kotz et al. describe ways to measure performance. The paper presents potential performance benefits of mobile agents in a typical data-filtering scenario. The scenario is based on a filtering experiment conducted during a U.S. Navy Fleet Battle Experiment. There mobile agents are used to jump across a wireless connection into the Internet to analyze intelligence databases. They filter incoming intelligence reports to find and return those reports with relevant information for the mission of a special battleship.

Benefits for mobile agent use in these environments include:

- Agents can select, scan, and filter incoming intelligence reports and forward only those that correlate to the significant event.
- The mobile scout agents stay at the remote information sources and only monitor new information. That reduces bandwidth and operator attention to irrelevant data.
- The mobile agents can act in the network outage. When the satellite connection is disconnected, the agents can filter information and buffer the reports.
- The number of scout agents can be increased very quickly, if needed.

To compare different approaches, two performance metrics, the bandwidth and the computation required, have been used. These performance metrics allow for the evaluation of the needed capacity in the server and in the network.

For the measurement of the performance, the following pipeline model has been used. In a time interval t, chunks of data are accumulated in the network buffer, are processed on the server, are being transmitted across the wireless network, and are being processed by the clients. For a stable pipeline, each stage must be able to complete its processing of data in less time than t.

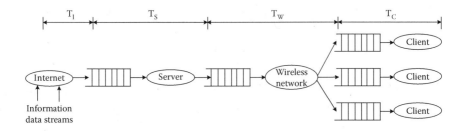

FIGURE 3.3 The mobile agent's data flow scenario as a pipeline.

Following Figure 3.3, the time to process the data at all positions has to be like the following:

- The time for transmission across the Internet to the server $T_I \le t$.
- The time for processing on the server $T_S \le t$.
- The time for transmission across the wireless network $T_W \le t$.
- The time processing on the client $T_C \le t$.

Most of these measured times have two variants for the agent case and for the broadcast case. For a detailed overview about all formulas see Kotz et al. (2002). The following formulas are examples of the ones presented by Kotz et al. and focus on the agent's part:

$$T_I = \frac{D}{B_I} \tag{3.2}$$

where D is the size of the data arriving during time period t, and B_I is the bandwidth available in the server's wired Internet connection.

$$T_S = \sum_{i=1}^{n} \sum_{j=1}^{m_i} \frac{c_{ij}(D, F'_{ij}, F_{ij})}{\alpha^S S^S} + \frac{rtC_{init}}{\alpha^S S^S}, \tag{3.3}$$

where c_{ij} is the computational complexity of task j on client i, F'_{ij} is the fraction of the total data D processed by task j on client i, F_{ij} is the fraction of the data processed by task j on client i, r is the arrival rate of new agents uploaded from the clients to the server, t is the time interval, c_{init} is the average number of operations needed for a new agent to start and exit, α^S is the performance efficiency of the software platform on the server, and S^S is the performance of the server machine.

$$T_W = \frac{\sum_{i,j} D, F'_{ij}, F_{ij}}{B_a}, \tag{3.4}$$

where B_a is the effective bandwidth available for agent messages.

In the agent's case, $T_C = 0$, because there are no data to be filtered on the client.

When measuring the mobile agents in a model, Kotz et al. use the Dartmouth mobile agent system as an example of a canonical mobile agent platform. They measure α^S, β, and C_{init} in example environments with special model parameters and present the results in a different manner.

In this case, the communication overhead factor β is for the broadcast of the agent with

$$\beta = \frac{B_a}{B}, \tag{3.5}$$

where B_a is the effective bandwidth available for the broadcast or for agent messages (bits/s), and B is the wireless channel's total physical bandwidth (bits/s).

The extensive measurement intentions of this work cannot be presented here, and so the authors only provide a first overview about the use of performance measurement in the area of mobile agents.

3.2.9 PERFORMANCE MEASURING IN LARGE NETWORKS BY WIJATA

An example with JATLite measurement agents for performance measuring in large networks is presented in Wijata, Niehaus, and Frost (2000). Based on the JATLite software agent's infrastructure, a system to control, collect, and monitor network information has been built. Figure 3.4 presents an overview about the agent-based measurement system. The JATLite-based system measures the round-trip time between specified network nodes to support the measurement of dynamic changes in the network.

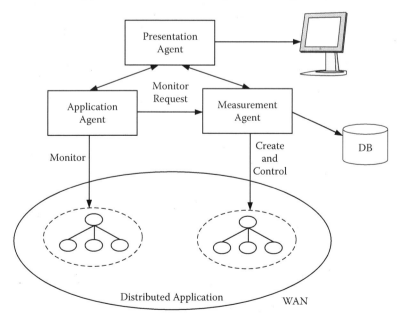

FIGURE 3.4   Relationships among agents in a network performance measurement system.

The collected real-time data can be used to monitor the network capability. The network agent performs network-level monitoring, and the presentation agent visualizes the state of the network as a front-end applet. The application agent monitors the status and the configuration of the application.

3.2.10   RPC Performance by Kotz et al.

Based on Agent Tcl, a mobile-agent system whose agents can be written in Tcl, the mobility of Remote Procedure Calls (RPCs) is defined in Kotz et al. (1997), which is created by an *Agent Interface Definition Language* (AIDL). Based on some prototypes, *RPC performance* is measured as the sum of the *client stub time, server stub time*, and *communication times*. In this case, the *client stub time* is the time to pack the procedure parameters into a byte stream, and the *server stub time* is the time to unpack the parameters. *Communication time* is the time to make a local procedure call with the same data.

Kotz et al. measured the performance of agent RPC using two machines. One was a 200 MHz Intel Pentium running Linux and the second was a 100 MHz Intel Pentium running FreeBsd version 2.1. Both computers were connected with a 10 Mbps Ethernet card. The measurement shows that the time to make an RPC is significantly smaller when both agents are on the same machine. If client and server are not on the same machine, it can take up to 200 times longer than the local call. Because communication costs 23% to 43% of the total time of execution, Kotz explains that Tcl is too slow.

3.2.11   Further Performance Evaluations

Further formulas to estimate the *response time* and the *time of delay* to notify, delete, create, and commit of software agents (see also Dikaiakos and Samaras 1999; Dumke and Wille 2001; Guichard and Ayel 1995; Kim and Cho 2003; Wille, Dumke, and Stojanov 2001) are defined in Evans et al. (1999).

3.2.12   Influences of the Knowledge Granularity on
the Agent Performance by Ye and Tsotsos

A formal description of different knowledge granularities is given in Ye and Tsotsos (2001), considering action pyramids in order to analyze different effects on the performance of the software agent behavior. Ye and Tsotsos's experiments show the influences of knowledge granularity on the overall performance of agents. Different examples show that a higher knowledge granularity attains a better quality of the selected action. For the performance of an agent, Ye and Tsotsos identify the following influences:

- The execution time.
- The action selection time.
- The total time constraint for the given task.
- The quality of the selected and executed action.

If the time needed to execute an action is very long, then it is worth spending more time to select good actions. However, if the time needed to execute an action is very short, it may not be beneficial to spend a lot of time on action selection, because this amount of time can be used to execute all the possible actions.

The given experiments show that the level of knowledge granularity has a big impact on the quality and speed of the agent's behavior. In some situations, it is possible to select the best knowledge granularity to maximize the performance of the agent. In the given example, an agent has to collect food in a defined region. In the closed example, the performance of the agent is measured by the total amount of food collected by the agent. In some situations, an agent is able to identify the optimal knowledge granularity based on task requirements and environment characteristics. The basic method is to try to represent the performance of the agent as a function of the agent's knowledge granularity and then to find the granularity that maximizes the performance. In practice, it is very difficult or even impossible to find the best knowledge granularity for an agent, because the performance of the agent might be influenced by many other factors in addition to the knowledge granularity.

3.2.13 UTILITY EVALUATION BY TEWARI AND MAES

A *user utility function modeling* in order to improve electronic markets is described in Tewari and Maes (2001). The implementation of a Buyer or Seller Valuation Manager (B/SVM) is based on some generic utility functions, such as:

$$UF_1 = (ax \pm b) \tag{3.6}$$

or

$$UF_5 = (ax^2 \pm bx \pm c) \tag{3.7}$$

Where x is a placeholder variable for a value of the flexible attribute over its permissible range, and a, b, and c represent arbitrary, nonnegative constants. Tewari and Maes initiate some first applications of this model.

3.2.14 USABILITY LEVEL DETERMINATION BY DEVELIN AND SCOTT

A speech technology agent and the usage of the two evaluation methods MUMMS (*Measuring the Usability of Multi-Media Software*) and TAM (*Technology Acceptance Model*) are considered in Devlin and Scott (2001). The factors that focus on usability are measured by questionnaires and groups of test users. The test users get a brief demonstration and description of the system, and time limits were imposed by the system. The following criteria are evaluated:

- Affect
- Control
- Efficiency

- Helpfulness
- Learnability
- Excitement

Devlin explained that the results are subjective in nature and more formal tests are needed. Further work should include a measurement of the *transaction completion time* and a comparative analysis of performance between different methods.

3.2.15 USABILITY MEASURES BY CABALLERO ET AL.

Examples for quantifiable usability measures are given in Caballero et al. (2003). These measurements include:

- The time a user (agent) takes to complete a task.
- The number of tasks of various kinds that can be completed within a given time limit.
- The ratio between successful interactions and errors.
- The time spent recovering from errors.
- The number of agent errors.

In the area of Web-based e-learning/e-teaching, an MAS as an intelligent tutoring system with different measurement agents is presented. The architecture of the agent system with different measurement agents and their interactions is presented in Figure 3.5.

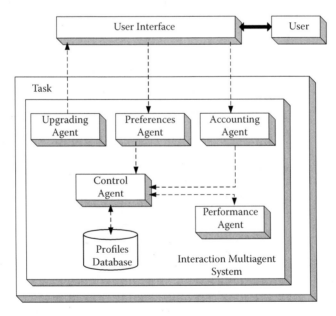

FIGURE 3.5   Measurement agents in a Web-based e-learning/e-teaching systems.

The following measurement agents can be identified:

- The *preference agent* perceives the interaction of the user with the user interface of the agent system and acts when the user changes his or her task.
- The *performance agent* calculates performance metrics when the user leaves the agent system.
- The *accounting agent* perceives the interaction between the user and the user interface of the agent system.
- The *upgrading agent* is constantly waiting for the *interaction control agent* to ask to update the user interface with new information.

The evaluation of the agent goals is an important consideration for agents required to behave autonomously in a real-world domain.

3.2.16 GOAL EVALUATION BY NORMAN AND LONG

Based on the Beliefs, Desires, and Intentions (BDI) architecture, Norman and Long (1995) describe a system of motivated goal creation (Figure 3.6). The agents get a triggering mechanism to control the relation between the current state and the predicted goal. The evaluation of the goal includes the conditions necessary for the goal to be satisfied and the importance of the goal. The threshold, weighted vector, and different trigging mechanism are discussed.

3.2.17 EVALUATION FUNCTION BY RUSSEL AND NORVIG

An example for an evaluation function that returns an estimation of the distance to the goal is given in Russel and Norvig (2003). An agent only performs well when it

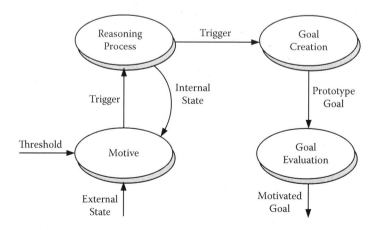

FIGURE 3.6 The motivated goal creation process (adapted from Norman and Long, 1995).

has a high-quality evaluation function. For the evaluation function of a game-playing agent, Russell presents the following design details:

- The evaluation function should order the terminal states in the same way as the true utility function.
- The computation must not take too long.
- For nonterminal states, the evaluation function should be strongly correlated with the actual chances to win.

Most evaluation functions work by calculating various features of the state. One way is to separate numerical contributions from each feature and afterward combine them to find the total value. One function called weighted linear function can be expressed as

$$EVAL(s) = w_1 f_1(s) + w_2 f_2(s) + \ldots + w_n f_{n1}(s) = \sum_{i=1}^{n} w_i f_i(s), \qquad (3.8)$$

where each w_i is a weight, and each f_i is a feature.

Analyzing different games like chess and backgammon, Russell defines additional criteria for evaluation functions (for example, an evaluation function must be a positive linear transformation of the probability of winning from the current position).

3.2.18 SUPPORT EVALUATION BY YANG AND CHOI

In the area of intelligent information extraction with agents, Yang and Choi (2003) introduce a *support value*. The support value increases whenever the ontology and the morphological pattern are matched with the document token scanned by the agent. Based on the support value, they can define a matching frequency to evaluate which pattern is useful to analyze the document.

3.2.19 FITNESS EVALUATION BY LOIA AND SESSA

Loia and Sessa (2001) characterize the agent fitness value deduced from the environment of the agent as the effect of a task execution. The fitness function appears as:

$$fitness = fitness_{t-1} + V_t \qquad (3.9)$$

V_t is a feedback value related to the time. V_t may be a positive value if the corresponding action has ameliorated the status of the agent or may be negative in the case of impoverishment of its state.

3.2.20 FITNESS EVALUATION BY LIU

During his research on self-organized behavior agents, Liu (2001, 2001a) discusses the agent's behavior adaptation and population control. Self-organized behavior agents can use a trigger function to control their own reproduction. The self-measured fitness value characterizes how many steps the agent needs to reach its goal.

$$f(A_i) = \left\{ 1 - \frac{\text{number of steps before reproduction}}{-1, \text{ life span of } A_i}, \right. \tag{3.10}$$

$f(A_i)$ denotes the fitness value of agent A_i.

Lee and Lee (2003) present a measurement approach based on the start time and finish time of subtasks performed by the agent to evaluate the *fitness* of an agent. In this approach, the start time of a subtask is affected by the finish time of the preceding subtask and the availability of required resources. Different functions to evaluate the fitness value are presented.

A *fitness function* is also described in the area of collective goal-directed task-driven behavior in a group of distributed agents. These agents, called ants, have to move an object by collective group handling. The fitness function is used to evolve an agent coordinated movement strategy and represents a high-level criterion for the task of collective object moving. The fitness function is defined as (Liu and Wu 2002):

$$S_f = s_1 \times s_2 \times s_3 \tag{3.11}$$

where s_1 specifies a net pushing force on an object as created by ants, which can be mathematically expressed as:

$$s_1 = \alpha \times \left\| \sum_i \vec{F_i} \right\| \tag{3.12}$$

where $\vec{F_i}$ is an artificial repulsive force on the object.

s_2 measures how close the agents are to the object, which is calculated as

$$s_2 = \lambda \times \left[\sum_i d_i \right]^{-1} \tag{3.13}$$

where d_i is the distance of the agent from the object to move.

Finally, s_3 indicates whether or not and how much the motion of the object is directed to a desired goal location:

$$s_3 = \left\{ \begin{array}{ll} \cos\theta & \theta \in \left[-\dfrac{\pi}{2}, \dfrac{\pi}{2} \right] \\ 0 & \textit{otherwise} \end{array} \right. \tag{3.14}$$

where θ is the direction of the group of agents. In the definition of the fitness function above, s_1 implies that the object should be pushed by a large net contact force, s_2

implies that the object should be moved toward a desired goal location, and s_3 implies that the rotation of the object should be discouraged during collective pushing.

3.2.21   Fitness Evaluation by Eymann

The fitness of agents in the area of e-commerce is presented in Eymann (2003). To find a successful market strategy, information about the efforts of different strategies is needed. The effort of a market strategy has to be measured and compared with other strategies with the help of MAS-based experiments. For Eymann, measurement of fitness in this background is described by how the agent can make successful transactions to increase its income. In the experiments, every agent starts with the same capital, and successful transactions increase the income. After a fixed amount of time cycles, it is possible to determine the agent with the best strategy.

A specific amount has to be paid in every time interval to the market manager so that every agent is forced to trade to increase its income. Agents with zero capital will be deleted from the experiment, and only the agents with the best strategy will survive. The fitness of an agent is the difference between the market price for the good and the subjective value of the traded product.

3.2.22   Service-Level Measurement by Bissel et al.

An example of using Zeus agents with measurement functionality for service-level management for e-mail is given in Bissel, Bonkowski, and Hadamschek (2004). Table 3.1 gives an overview of the tasks and boundary conditions measured by a team of agents presented in the example.

TABLE 3.1
Agent Tasks for E-mail Measurement

Task Type	Threshold
Measure establishment errors	Connection establishment time >8 min
Measure connection establishment time	≤2 min
Measure release errors	Connection release time ≥3 min
Measure connection release time	≤3 min
Measure transfer errors	Lost message per total number of errors ≤3%
Measure lost message per usage	≤3%
Measure transmission time	2 Mbps
Measure acknowledgement time	5 min
Measure number of recovered messages per disrupted messages	≥80% recovered messages per disrupted messages
Message recovery errors	≥80 %
Measure availability	24 hours / 7 days / 52 weeks

3.2.23 RESOURCE ALLOCATION SIMULATION BY BREDIN ET AL.

Based on a simulated market environment, Bredin et al. (2001) introduced an agent system where agents have the ability to assess the cost of their actions. The agent system as the environment, coordinates their resource addressed to time and space. The idea is to create a resource allocation policy for mobile agent systems and derive an algorithm for a mobile agent to plan its expenditure and travel. The goal is that accommodation of agents at hosts should be fair, and the information should allow the agents to optimally plan their time. To evaluate the algorithm, design simulations are used to test how the MAS can handle burst workloads, situations where network resources are overextended, so that the performance of the agents does not get catastrophically affected.

To reach this goal, a performance measure has been used. The idealized measure is the shortest path for an agent from the start host to visit hosts that offer services to complete the agent's itineraries. The edge lengths of the path are the sum of network transfer latencies from the previous host and the time required to process the job. After the network has reached a steady state, the performance of a single agent can be measured in a network with zero resource contention. The simulations show differences between the planning algorithms and it can also be shown that the performance of the agents decays gradually as the quality of their network information decreases. In the presented case, an MAS can be used as a decentralized method of flow control for network bandwidth by the auctioning of bandwidth.

3.2.24 COOPERATION MEASUREMENT BY KLUSCH AND SYCARA

Klusch and Sycara (2001) establish some empirical characteristics of agent cooperation and collaboration:

- The *level* and *intensity* of communication between software agents.
- The *kind* and the *quality* of coordination between interacting agents.
- The *intention* of collaboration as the basis of the evaluation of the agent efficiency.
- The *volume* and the *efficiency* of the cooperation.
- The *increase of the agent facilities* and knowledge during the collaboration.

One example of measurement in this area is shown in Section 3.2.36.

3.2.25 DISTRIBUTED DECISION MEASUREMENT OF COORDINATION BY BARBER

Barber, Han, and Liu (2000) consider five types of agent coordination: (1) arbitration, (2) negotiation, (3) mediation, (4) voting, and (5) self-modification. The different kinds of evaluation of these coordination types are based on the effort for *searching an agent, for voting,* and on the *voting effort.*

3.2.26 COALITION VALUE ESTIMATION BY SHEHORY ET AL.

Cooperation between autonomous agents is an important method in multiagent environments for maximizing the payoffs of single agents (Shehory, Sycara, and Jha 1997). In the area of strategic coalition between agents, Yang and Choi (2003b) describes a *coalition value*. The strategic coalition can be formed among agents like $C = \{C_i, C_j, \ldots, C_k\}$, $|C| \geq 2$. The coalition is the element of the individual group $I : C \subseteq I, |I|$. Every agent has its own payoff p_i. The coalition has the vector $C = (S_c, N_c, F_P, D_c)$ with the following description:

- S_c = the sum of the coalition payoff
- N_c = the number of agents in the coalition
- f_P = payoff function
- D_c = decision of the function
- w = weight vector of each agent
- C_p = the coalition value as the average payoff by the corresponding confidence of agents that participate in the coalition

The coalition value is given as:

$$C_p = \frac{S_c}{|C|} \tag{3.15}$$

where

$$w_i = \frac{p_i}{\displaystyle\sum_{i=1}^{|C|} p_i} \tag{3.16}$$

and

$$S_c = \sum_{i=1}^{|C|} p_i * w_i \tag{3.17}$$

3.2.27 COMMUNICATION INDEX BY PEDRYCZ AND VOKOVICH

The quality of an existing communication process between agents is defined by Pedrycz and Vokovich (2001):

$$Comm\_index(X, A_1, A_2, \ldots, A_c) = C - \sum_{i=1}^{C} (Poss(X, A_i)) \tag{3.18}$$

where X is the input information granule; $A_1, A_2, \ldots, A_C$ is the collection of information granules specific to the agent; and $Poss(X, A_i)$ is the possibility measure of communication.

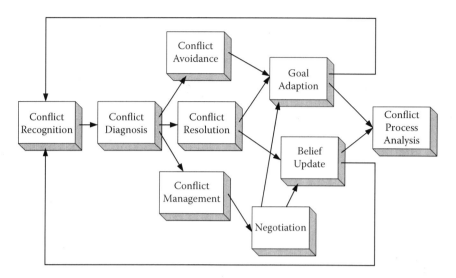

FIGURE 3.7 Conflict-handling action model.

We will demonstrate these general aspects in Figure 3.7, which describes the general conflict handling of software agents (see Tessier, Chaudron, and Müller 2001).

The conflict diagnosis and conflict management should be covered by measures or metrics in order to achieve the goal adaptation and to improve the conflict process analysis. Such metrics depend on characteristic data of the negotiation contents and processes.

3.2.28 INTELLIGENCE FACTORS BY HASEBROOK ET AL.

Knowbots as self-learning agents in an MAS are described in Hasebrook, Erasmus, and Doeben-Henisch (2002). The distributed computational intelligence can be used to help people gain control in the fast-growing information universe. During a discussion about what intelligence is and how the intelligence of a machine can be measured, Hasebrook and colleagues describe a mathematical representation of intelligence factors (*IF*). Not all of these intelligence factors are known today, but mathematically they are include:

$$Intelligence \subseteq \bigcup IF_i \qquad (3.19)$$

Thus, the intelligence quotient (*IQ*) is then defined as:

$$IQ \leq \int_{intelligence} m(IF) \qquad (3.20)$$

where $m(IF)$ is defined to measure the intelligence factor quotient (*IFQ*) of *IF*. Thus, in general, it can be stated that:

$$IQ \leq \sum IFQ_i \qquad (3.21)$$

In a special case where the different intelligence factors are mutually exclusive, it can be said that:

$$IQ = \int_{intelligence} m(IF), \text{ or } IQ = \sum IFQ_i \qquad (3.22)$$

Following this definition of an intelligence factor, it will be possible to measure the intelligence of agents or agent-based systems. Unfortunately, not all intelligence factors are known today, and so there is no chance for successfully measuring such a system. One of the known intelligence factors is the ability to learn, and in a general sense, it can be said that when an agent is intelligent, it should be able to learn.

3.2.29 TRUST MEASUREMENT BY CHANG ET AL.

Chang, Hussain, and Dillon (2005) present the CCCI (Correlation, Commitment, Clarity, and Influence) methodology to measure the trustworthiness of agents in business interactions. This trustworthiness measure can be defined as the measure of the trust level or the trustworthiness value of the agent. The proposed values can be used as criteria whether or not to interact with the special agent. To measure, Chang, Hussain, and Dillon defined four metrics. The fulfillment of a commitment $Commit_{Criterion}$ measures how much of the criterion defined in the service agreement has been fulfilled by the delivered service. Therefore, seven levels are defined (–1 to 5). The clarity of each criterion $Clear_{Criterion}$ and $Inf_{Criterion}$ is also ordinal defined (–1 to 7) and describes the clarity and influence of each commitment of the service agreement. After all, trustworthiness T is measured as:

$$T = 5 * \frac{\sum_{c=1}^{N} Commit_{Criterion\_c} * Clear_{Criterion\_c} * Inf_{Criterion\_c}}{\sum_{c=1}^{N} 5 * Clear_{Criterion\_c} * Inf_{Criterion\_c}} \qquad (3.23)$$

Using the metric, the authors present an ordinal scale with seven levels to present trustworthiness (–1 to 5) meaning:

1. Unknown Agent
2. Very Untrustworthy
3. Untrustworthy
4. Partially Trustworthy
5. Largely Trustworthy
6. Trustworthy
7. Very Trustworthy

3.2.30 PERFORMANCE ESTIMATION AND MEASUREMENT OF COMPUTATIONAL AGENTS BY NERUDA AND KRUSINA

Run-time analysis of complex parallel asynchronous processes is presented in Neruda and Krusina (2005). The authors implemented a genetic algorithm using an MAS. For a parallel execution, they decomposed the algorithm (Figure 3.8).

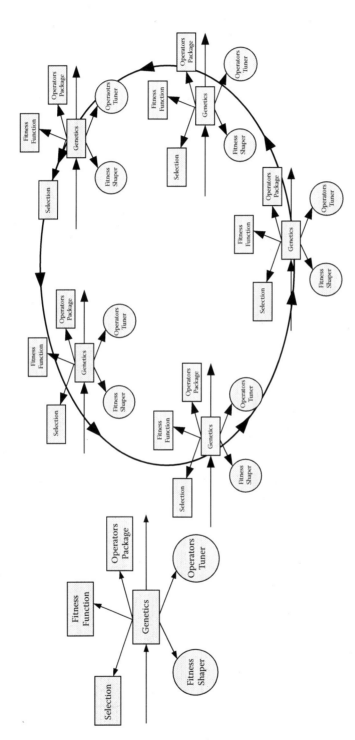

FIGURE 3.8 (Left) The generalized genetic algorithm decomposition. (Right) The generalized genetic algorithm parallelization via circular communication among per-machine subpopulations.

They predicted and afterward measured the iteration times needed by the genetic algorithm on four different hardware architectures. Measured properties are integer operations, floating point operations, processor cycles, number and type of communication, and the size of transferred data.

3.2.31   AGENT-BASED IP MEASUREMENT BY KWITT ET AL.

Kwitt et al. (2006) described a modular architecture for Internet Protocol (IP) measurement in classic network and wireless scenarios. It is based on an MAS containing management and measurement agents developed with the JAVA Agent Development Framework (JADE) environment. The tool's architecture is visualized in Figure 3.9.

The management agent periodically checks a database for new measurement jobs to distribute them to the specific measurement agents. Newly started agents register themselves at the management agent with their capabilities and specific parameters.

Possible measurement scenarios include:

- *Active flow measurement*: Active traffic generation and measurement
- *Passive measurement*: Passive observation
- *Perceptual measurement*: Determination of an overall quality value

3.2.32   AGENT-BASED METRIC FOR WIRELESS NETWORKS BY CHEN AND CHEN

In a scenario of a needed central framework for the quality of service improvement in wireless networks, an agent-based metric is proposed in Chen and Chen (2006). The Anticipative Agent Assistance (AAA) evaluates and manages wireless access points (APs) and provides quality information to clients. Based on these data, the user may adjust the service quality in terms of throughput and delay requirements.

A central server agent manages network resources with the help and information of client agents that are installed on the access points. The used algorithm sorts available APs according to their load and distance to the mobile user. Now the needed information is available for mobile user movement and AP-switching in order to improve the quality of service.

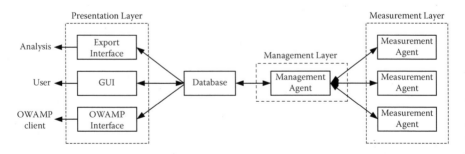

FIGURE 3.9   Infrastructure of the IP measurement by Kwitt. (GUI: graphic user interface.)

The authors performed evaluations with the following results:

- Reduction of transmission delay
- Increase of throughput
- Improvement of overall network utilization
- Accommodation of more users
- Provision of load balancing

3.2.33 REPLICATION-BASED AGENT OPTIMIZATION BY GUESSOUM

For certain replication-based optimization approaches, Guessoum, Faci, and Briot (2005) define a criticality metric for an agent. It is based on interdependencies with other agents that can be described as weights in a label-oriented graph. Using this criticality, they compute the number of replicas nb_i of Agent$_i$:

$$nb_i = rounded(rm + w_i * \frac{Rm}{W})$$
(3.24)

with w_i as the agent's criticality, W as the sum of the domain agent's criticality, a manually predefined minimum number of replicas rm, and RM as the maximum number of replicas.

An interesting measurement result of their experiments is that the monitoring effort is a constant function. The authors' arguments are based on the hierarchical nature of their agent's organization. By this the communication is optimized, because it happens only in case of local changes.

Furthermore, the authors present adaptation mechanisms to dynamically and automatically update the strategy used to replicate the most critical agents.

3.2.34 COMMUNICATION LEARNING FOR AGENT COMMUNICATION BY FISCHER ET AL.

With an increasing degree of openness in MAS, standard communication approaches like agent communication languages (ACLs) may no longer be sufficient. Fischer, Rovatsos, and Weiss (2005) deal with this problem and use methods from case-based reasoning, inductive logic programming, and cluster analysis. The goal is to enable agents to autonomously create and maintain a model of different classes of conversation. Therefore, an initial ACL and protocol set are needed.

For the formal scheme, distance metrics are proposed to measure the distance between message sequences and between frames in agent communication. The first metric without further explanation is presented below:

$$d(m,n) = \frac{1}{|m|+1} \sum_{i=1}^{|m|} d(m_i,n_i), \quad \text{if } m = n; 1 \text{ otherwise}$$
(3.25)

3.2.35 PERFORMANCE OF MOBILE AGENT TRACKING BY GÓMEZ-MARTÍNEZ ET AL.

Gómez-Martínez, Ilarri, and Merseguer (2007) analyze the performance of tracking mobile agents in a distributed computing environment. They do not perform experiments but instead use the predicting urbanization with multiagents (PUMA) approach. Based on a design model (for example, UML), it allows the extraction of a target performance model. Within the presented paper, the authors create a generalized stochastic petri net (GSPN) that is the basis for the computation of the response time metric. The main result is that the response time increases linearly.

An interesting time measure for basic operations of mobile agents within the agent platform is SPRINGS (Scalable PlatfoRm for movING Software) and is presented by the authors in Table 3.2. The computers used are Pentium IV 1.7 GHz with Linux RedHat 2.4.18 and 256 MBytes RAM.

3.2.36 EFFICIENCY OF CHOSEN MEASUREMENT AGLET AGENTS BY WILLE

In his work, Wille (2005) describes different measurement agents based on Aglet software agents. A detailed overview of the measurement Aglets at the Otto-von-Guericke University of Magdeburg is presented in Wille, Dumke, and Stojanov (2001); Müller (2001); Dumke and Wille (2001); and Wille, Dumke, and Stojanov (2002a), and an overview is given in Figure 3.10.

TABLE 3.2
Times of Basic System Execution Operations for One Mobile Agent

Operation	Mean Execution Time (ms)
preDeparture	0.1
postDeparture	0.1
preArrival	0.1
postArrival	0.1
CreateAgent	43.82
RemoveAgent	3.86
SendAgent	46.3
RegistryAgent	13.14
UnregistryAgent	3.86
UpdateProxies	20.2
RequestCall	0.1
CallAgent	9.3
AskLocation	20
FindProxy	32
UpdateProxyList	1.0

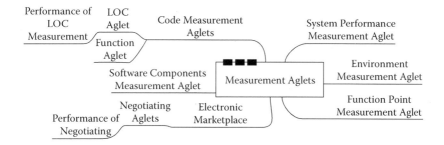

FIGURE 3.10 Overview of existing measurement Aglets.

Therefore, the author identified agent performance (AP) aspects that are described below. The descriptions are given in alphabetical order.

- *Adaptation performance AP*$_{adaptation}$: The adaptation performance quantifies the time effort for the migration of the software agent intentions in order to keep further tasks in the agent-based system: $AP_{adaptationt} = s_{intentions}$.
- *Collaboration performance AP*$_{collaboration}$: The collaboration performance determines the part of service time of the common tasks that were realized with other agents: $AP_{collaboration} = a_{commonTasks} \times s_{commonTasks}$.
- *Communication performance AP*$_{communication}$: The communication performance will be expressed by the average time of message sending and receiving in order to work on a common task between agents: $AP_{communication} = s_{messages}$.
- *Cooperation performance AP*$_{cooperation}$: The cooperation performance will be executed through the average time effort for task realization of an agent relating to the other agents participating in the task: $AP_{cooperation} = s_{commonTasks}$.
- *Coordination performance AP*$_{coordination}$: The coordination performance is caused by the average time effort of the coordination between the agents in order to work on a common task: $AP_{coordination} = s_{controlTasks}$.
- *Interaction performance AP*$_{interaction}$: The interaction performance characterizes the time to reply during the interaction of the software agent relating to the user interface: $AP_{interaction} = r$.
- *Learning performance AP*$_{learning}$: The learning performance executes the effort for extension and adaptation of the knowledge of a software agent: $AP_{learning} = s_{knowledge}$.
- *Mobility performance AP*$_{mobility}$: The mobility performance determines the average dwell time of an agent in the visited cities: $AP_{mobility} = s_{system-basedTasks}$.
- *Negotiation performance AP*$_{negotiation}$: The negotiation performance determines the average time effort for the preparation and coordination of a task solution between software agents: $AP_{negotiation} = s_{intentionalTasks}$.
- *Operation performance AP*$_{operation}$: The operation performance executes the average time effort for the realization of the agent tasks/operations: $AP_{operation} = s_{tasks}$.

- *Reproduction performance AP*$_{reproduction}$: The reproduction performance is addressed to the effort of the regeneration or reproduction of the system-based operations of a software agent: $AP_{reproduction} = s_{regenerationTasks}$.
- *Suitability performance AP*$_{suitability}$: The suitability performance evaluates the loss of efficiency caused by redundancy in the functionality of a software agent addressed to the problem solution:

$$AP_{suitability} = (c - a) \times s_{commonTasks}. \tag{3.26}$$

3.2.37   WORKBENCH FOR AGENT RESOURCE USAGE ANALYSIS BY WILLE

To become a part of mainstream software development, agent-oriented software development has to demonstrate its capabilities. In case of performance engineering, the use of resources by software agents and MAS has to be analyzed. How do MAS resource requirements compare with other MAS or applications? Are there any bottlenecks during the use of the MAS? Until now, these questions could not be answered.

The AgentBench is a prototype that can be used to collect empirical measures. In the current version, the metrics used have been borrowed from traditional performance engineering and have focused system resources (Wille 2005).

The goal is to measure the resource allocation of different MASs during run-time and to minimize measurement deviations. In this case, AgentBench should not be a part of the MAS and runs as its own application. The first intention to get the measures from the Java Virtual Machine (JVM) was not useful, and so the measures are taken from the working system. After starting and calibrating AgentBench, the duration time for measurement, the measurement interval, and the name of the log file can be set. The calibration will minimize the influences from other applications.

An overview of the placement of AgentBench on the system and a screenshot of the start-up screen are shown in Figure 3.11.

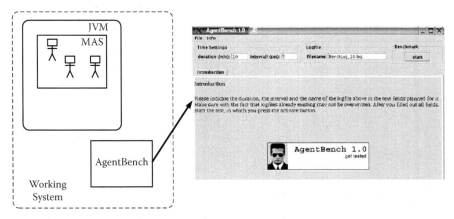

FIGURE 3.11   Placement and starting view of AgentBench.

3.3 DISCUSSION

Based on the reviews of hundreds of sources, essential quality measurement intentions in the area of software agents were found. Shown in Figure 3.12 is an overview of the agent quality criteria that have been found.

With the more quantitative overview, it can be established that most measurement goals can be categorized as performance measurement, fitness measurement, and communication measurement. This result is clear, because the developer wants to know how well agents perform in a particular area of use. In relation to the task that the agent has to perform, the interpretation of performance can be very different: on one hand, the time that an agent needs to satisfy the task, and on the other, the profit of a negotiating agent in an electronic marketplace. Additionally, the border between performance of an agent and its fitness is not clear. Sometimes fitness and performance cover the same area of measurement.

The inventory of agent-related measurement research approaches published over the last year shows that some criteria have not yet been measured (for example, portability, security, trustworthiness, reusability, functionality, testability, and efficiency).

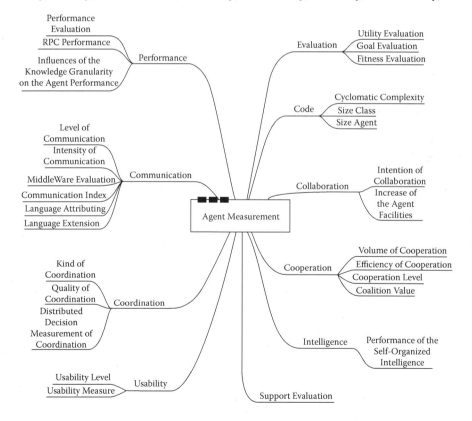

FIGURE 3.12 General overview about the usage of measurement in the area of software agents.

REFERENCES

Barber, K. S., D. C. Han, and T. H. Liu. 2000. Co-ordinating Distributed Decision Making Using Reusable Interaction Specification. In *Design and Applications of Intelligent Agents*, ed. C. Zhang and V. W. Soo, 1–15. Berlin: Springer.

Bissel, T., C. Bonkowski, and V. Hadamschek. 2004. Service Level Management with Agent Technology. Working Paper, www.mnlab.cs.depaul.edu/seminar/fall2001/SLMAgent.pdf (accessed January 5, 2009).

Bredin, J., D. Kotz, D. Rus, R. T. Maheswaran, C. Imer, and T. Basar. 2001. A Market-Based Model for Resource Allocation in Agent Systems. In *Coordination of Internet Agents Models, Technologies, and Applications,* ed. A. Omincini, F. Zambonelli, M. Klusch, and R. Tolksdorf, 426–442. Berlin: Springer.

Caballero, A. F., V. L. Jaquero, F. Montero, and P. Gonzalez. 2003. Adaptive Interaction Multi-Agent Systems in E-Learning/E-Teaching on the Web. In *Proceedings of the Web Engineering International Conference (ICWE 2003)*, ed. J. M. C. Lovelle, B. M. G. Rodriguez, J. E. L. Gayo, and M. P. P. Ruiz, 144–153. Berlin: Springer.

Chang, E., F. K. Hussain, and T. Dillon. 2005. CCCI Metrics for the Measurement of Quality of E-Service. In *Proceedings of the IEEE/WIC/ACM International Conference on Intelligent Agent Technology (IAT 2005)*, ed. F. Compiegne et al., 603–610. Los Altimos, CA: IEEE Computer Society Press.

Chen, Y. -C. and W. -Y. Chen. 2006. An Agent-Based Metric for Quality of Service over Wireless Networks. In *Proceedings of the 2006 Annual International Computer Software and Applications Conference (COMPSAC 2006)*, ed. A. Elci and M. T. Kone, 236–246. Los Altimos: IEEE Computer Society Press.

Devlin, M. and T. Scott. 2001. Using a Speech Technology Agent as an Interface for E-Commerce. In *E-Commerce Agents*, ed. J. Liu and Y. Ye, 332–346. Berlin: Springer.

Dikaiakos, M. D. and G. Samaras. 1999. Performance Evaluation of Mobile Agents: Issues and Approaches. In *Performance Engineering*, Lecture Notes in Computer Science 2047, ed. R. Dumke, C. Rautenstrauch, A. Schmietendorf, and A. Scholz, 148–166. New York: Springer.

Dumke, R. 2000. Experience-Based Applications of a General Object-Oriented Measurement Framework (German). In *Software-Metriken*, ed. R. Dumke and F. Lehner, 71–93. Wiesbaden: Deutscher Universitätsverlag.

Dumke, R. and C Wille. 2001. Performance Engineering for Software Agents (German). In *Proceedings of the 2. Workshop Performance Engineering*, ed. A. Schmietendorf, A. Scholz, R. Dumke, and C. Rautenstrauch, 33–46. Magdeburg: University Press.

Evans, R., F. Sommers, D. Kerr, and D. O'Sullivan. 1999. A Multi-Agent System Architecture for Scalable Management of High Performance Networks: Applying Arms Length Autonomy. In *Software Agents for Future Communication Systems*, ed. A. L. G. Hayzelden and J. Bigham, 86–111. New York: Springer.

Eymann, T. 2003. *Digital Business Agents* (German). Berlin: Springer.

Fischer, F., M. Rovatsos, and G. Weiss. 2005. Acquiring and Adapting Probabilistic Models of Agent Conversation. In *Proceedings of the 4th International Joint Conference on Autonomous Agents and Multi-Agent Systems (AAMAS 2005)*, ed. F. Dignum et al., 106–113. Utrecht, Netherlands: Utrecht University Press.

Gómez-Martínez, E., S. Ilarri, and J. Merseguer. 2007. Performance Analysis of Mobile Agents Tracking. In *Proceedings of 6th International Workshop on Software and Performance (WOSP 2007)*, ed. V. Cortellessa and S. Uchitel, 181–188. Los Altimos, CA: IEEE Computer Society Press.

Guessoum, Z., N. Faci, and J. -P. Briot. 2005. Adaptive Replication of Large-Scale Multi-Agent Systems — Towards a Fault-Tolerant Multi-Agent Platform. In *Software Engineering for Large-Scale Multi-Agent Systems (SELMAS 2005)*, ed. E. Garcia et al., 238–253. Los Altimos, CA: IEEE Computer Society Press.

Guichard, F. and J. Ayel. 1995. Logical Reorganization of DAI Systems. In *Intelligent Agents*, ed. M. J. Wooldridge and N. R. Jennings, 118–128. Berlin: Springer.

Hasebrook, J., L. Erasmus, and G. Doeben-Henisch. 2002. Knowledge Robots for Knowledge Workers: Self-Learning Agents Connecting Information and Skills. In *Intelligent Agents and Their Applications*, ed. L. C. Jain, Z. Chen, and N. Ichalkaranje, 59–81. Heidelberg: Physica.

Jennings, N. R. and M. J. Wooldridge. 1998. *Agent Technology — Foundation, Applications and Markets*. New York: Springer.

Joshi, A., N. Ramakrishnan, and E. N. Houstis. 1998. Multi-Agent System Support of Networked Scientific Computing. *Internet Computing* 2(3): 69–83.

Kim, J. K. and Y. H. Cho. 2003. Using Web Usage Mining and SVD to Improve E-commerce Recommendation Quality. In *Intelligent Agents and Multi-Agent Systems 6th Pacific Rim International Workshop on Multi-Agents (PRIMA 2003)*, 86–97. Berlin: Springer.

Klusch, M. and K. Sycara. 2001. Brokering and Matchmaking for Coordination of Agent Societies: A Survey. In *Coordination of Internet Agents Models, Technologies, and Applications*, ed. A. Omincini, F. Zambonelli, M. Klusch, and R. Toksdorf, 197–224. Berlin: Springer.

Kotz, D., R. Gray, S. Nog, D. Rus, S. Chawla, and G. Cybenko. 1997. Agent TCL: Targeting the Needs of Mobile Agents. *Internet Computing* 1(3): 58–67.

Kotz, D., G. Cybenko, R. Gray, G. Jiang, R. A. Peterson, M. O. Hofmann, D. A. Chacon, K. R. Whitebread, and J. Hendler. 2002. Performance Analysis of Mobile Agents for Filtering Data Streams on Wireless Networks. *Mobile Networks and Applications* 7(2): 163–174.

Kwitt, R., T. Fichtel, T. Pfeiffenberger, and U. Hofmann. 2006. A New Agent-Based Approach towards Distributed IP Measurements. In *Proceedings of the International Conference on Networking, International Conference on Systems and International Conference on Mobile Communications and Learning Technologies (ICNICONSMCL 2006)*, ed. B. Zhao and C. Liu, 52–59. Los Altimos, CA: IEEE Computer Society Press.

Lee, K. M. and J. H. Lee. 2003. Coordinated Collaboration of Multiagent Systems Based on Generic Algorithms. In *Intelligent Agents and Multi-Agent Systems 6th Pacific Rim International Workshop on Multi-Agents (PRIMA 2003)*, ed. J. Lee and M. Barley, 145–156. Heidelberg: Springer.

Liu, J. 2001. *Autonomous Agents and Multi-Agent Systems — Explorations in Learning, Self-Organization and Adaptive Computation*. Singapore: World Scientific.

Liu, J. 2001a. Self-Organized Intelligence. In *Agent Engineering*, ed. J. Liu, N. Zhong, Y. Y. Tang, and P. S. P. Wang, 123–148. Singapore: World Scientific.

Liu, J. and J. Wu. 2002. Collective Behavior Evolution in a Group of Cooperating Agents. In *Intelligent Agents and Their Applications*, ed. L. C. Jain, Z. Chen, and N. Ichalkaranje, 173–216. Heidelberg: Physica.

Loia, V. and S. Sessa. 2001. A Soft Computing Framework for Adaptive Agents. In *Soft Computing Agents: New Trends for Designing Autonomous Systems*, ed. V. Loia and S. Sessa, 191–220. Heidelberg: Physica.

Müller, J. 2001. Modeling and Prototypical Implementation of Quality Evaluation of Agent-Based Software Systems (German). Diploma Thesis. Department of Computer Science, University of Magdeburg, Germany.

Neruda, R. and P. Krusina. 2005. Estimating and Measuring Performance of Computational Agents. In *The 2005 IEEE/WIC/ACM International Conference on Intelligent Agent Technology (IAT 2005)*, ed. A. Compiegne et al., 615–618. Los Altimos, CA: IEEE Computer Society Press.

Norman, T. J. and D. Long. 1995. Goal Creation in Motivated Agents. In *Intelligent Agents*, ed. M. J. Wooldridge and N. R. Jennings, 277–290. Berlin: Springer.

Pedrycz, W. and G. Vokovich. 2001. Intelligent Agents in Granular Worlds. In *Soft Computing Agents*, ed. V. Loia and S. Sessa, 47–71. Heidelberg: Physica.

Pham, H. H. 2002. Software Agents for Internet-Based System and Their Design. In *Intelligent Agents and Their Applications*, L. C. Jain, Z. Chen, and N. Ichalkaranje, 101–147. Heidelberg: Physica.

Russell, S. J. and P. Norvig. 2003. *Artificial Intelligence: A Modern Approach,* 2nd ed. Upper Saddle River, NJ: Prentice Hall.

Shehory, O., K. Sycara, and S. Jha. 1997. Multi-agent Coordination through Coalition Formation. In *Intelligent Agents IV: Agent Theories, Architectures and Languages,* Lecture Notes in Artificial Intelligence, Springer 1365, ed. M. P. Singh, A. Rao, and M. J. Wooldridge, 143–154. Berlin: Springer.

Sugawara, S., K. Yamaoka, and Y. Sakai. 2001. Efficient Means of Resource Discovery Using Agents. In *Agent Technology for Communication Infrastructures,* ed. A. L. G. Hayzelden and R. A. Bourne, 275–286. Chichester: John Wiley & Sons.

Sycara, K., M. Paolucci, M. Van Velsen, and J. Giampapa. 2003. The RETSINA MAS Infrastructure. *Autonomous Agents and Multi-Agent Systems* 7: 29–48.

Tambe, M., D. V. Pynadath, and N. Chauvat. 2000. Building Dynamic Agent Organizations in Cyberspace. *IEEE Internet Computing* 4(2): 65–73.

Tessier, C., L. Chaudron, and H. J. Müller. 2001. *Conflicting Agents — Conflict Management in Multi-Agent Systems.* Boston: Kluwer Academic.

Tewari, G. and P. Maes. 2001. A Generalized Platform for Specification, Valuation, and Brokering of Heterogeneous Resources in Electronic Markets. In *E-Commerce Agents*, ed. J. Liu and Y. Ye, 7–24. Berlin: Springer.

Wijata, Y. I., D. Niehaus, and V. S. Frost. 2000. A Scalable Agent-Based Network Measurement Infrastructure. *IEEE Communications* 38(9): 174–183.

Wille, C., R. Dumke, and S. Stojanov. 2001. Performance Engineering in Agent-Based Systems — Concepts, Modelling and Examples. In *Current Trends in Software Measurement*, ed. R Dumke and A. Abran, 153–184. Aachen, Germany: Shaker.

Wille, C., R. Dumke, and S. Stojanov. 2002. Quality Assurance in Agent-Based Systems Current State and Open Problems. Preprint No. 4, Department of Computer Science, University of Magdeburg, Germany.

Wille, C., R. Dumke, and S. Stojanov. 2002a. Software Measurement and Evaluation of Agent-Based System Development and Application (German). In *Software Messung und -Bewertung*, ed. R. Dumke and D. Rombach, 219–253. Wiesbaden: Deutscher Universitätsverlag.

Wille, C. 2005. Agent Measurement Framework. Ph.D. Thesis, University of Magdeburg, Germany.

Yang, J. and J. Choi. 2003. Agents for Intelligent Information Extraction by Using Domain Knowledge and Token-Based Morphological Patterns. In *Intelligent Agents and Multi-Agent Systems 6th Pacific Rim International Workshop on Multi-Agents (PRIMA 2003),* ed. J. Lee and M. Barley, 74–97. Berlin: Springer.

Ye, Y. and J. K. Tsotsos. 2001. Knowledge Granulary Spectrum, Action Pyramid, and the Scaling Problem. In *Agent Engineering*, ed. J. Liu, N. Zhong, Y. Y. Tang, and P. S. P. Wang, 29–58. Singapore: World Scientific.

4 Quality Measurement of Agent Systems

4.1 INTRODUCTION

The viewpoints of agent-based systems, especially multiagent systems (MASs), are generally defined in architectural models. First, let's begin with a general description of MAS aspects as shown in Figure 4.1.

The described MAS architecture includes some essential quality intentions using basic measurement methods including estimation, prediction, evaluation, management, and controlling. Note that all considered kinds of quality evaluation in previous chapters are also relevant to MAS evaluation. In this chapter, the additional quality aspects of agent-based systems will be described.

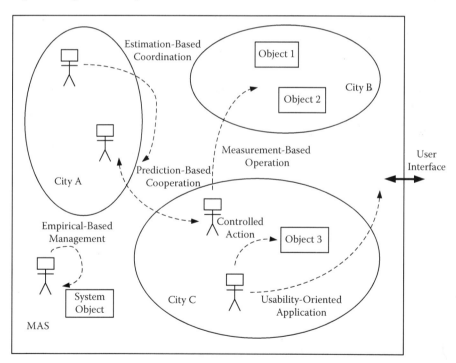

FIGURE 4.1 Measurement-based multiagent system architecture.

4.2 QUALITY MEASUREMENT APPROACHES OF A MULTIAGENT SYSTEM (MAS)

4.2.1 COMPARISON OF COMMUNICATION BY PHAM

Pham (2002) explained a comparison of different communication methods in the area of a MAS-based e-marketplace. For the comparison, he uses the criteria described in Table 4.1.

To compare methods like yellow pages, black board, contract-net, pattern-based, and peer-to-peer with their own model, Pham created agents from 10 to 100,000 with a fixed ratio between the number of agents and the number of requests. Setting the acceptable reliability of possible requests in an MAS to 90%, it was possible to find out how many agents the system can house. The differences for the observed system move from 300 agents with the communication method pattern-based, to 4000 agents with the communication methods yellow pages and contract-net. Under the given environment, the communication method yellow pages produces 90% of failure requests when the number of agents grows over 20,000.

4.2.2 COMMUNICATION QUALITY EVALUATION BY LUKSCHANDL

An example for MAS-based communication in communication networks is given by Lukschandl (2001). This work focuses on the routing problem in communication networks, especially the study of how to reduce the number of telephone calls that cannot be successfully connected due to congestion in one or more parts of the network. To evaluate his model, Lukschandl uses a simulation in a given network topology. During each run of the simulation, the following kinds of data are measured:

- The number of blocked calls.
- The number of circular calls.
- The value of successfully routed calls.

Different experiments were done, and one goal was to minimize the number of lost calls.

TABLE 4.1

Comparison Criteria for Communication Methods in Agent Systems

Criteria	Description
Average response time	Response time of all agents' requests divided by the number of requests. The response time for a request is the period of time from the moment when the request is made to the moment when it is known if it can result in a deal or not.
Reliability	This is the probability that the given system works without crash, in experiments it can be defined in percent as a ratio of number of times the system works without crash to the total number of runs.
Communication degree	Number of channels created in the agent communication system at a time.

The following function is used to calculate the c-resistance (R_c):

$$R_c = d + L \times \left(0,5 \times d + 2 + 0,5 \times d \times \left(d + L / (d - L^2)\right)\right) \tag{4.1}$$

with the distance (d) measured as the number of links and the current load of the node (L) measured as percent of the maximal load. In this experiment, the load is zero if the agents choose the shortest path.

4.2.3 RISK EVALUATION BY COLLINS ET AL.

At the University of Minnesota, a multiagent negotiation test bed (Magnet) system (Collins et al. 2001) was developed. This system is designed to support multiple agents in negotiation contracts for tasks with temporal and precedence constraints. The Magnet system market infrastructure supplies customer agents with statistics to help with decision making, connects customer and supplier agents, and helps the agent to communicate (Figure 4.2). The market infrastructure provides an ontology that describes all types of goods available in the market.

The Magnet test bed allows for the monitoring of agent functions like planning, negotiation, and execution, and supports the customer agents with market statistics.

To allow agents to make appropriate autonomous decisions, they must support a risk evaluation. The Magnet agent market maintains the following types of data on each supplier and task type:

- Performance of commitment (P_c) as the ratio of successful attempts where the task was completed within the promised duration.
- Performance with overruns (P_1) as the percentage of attempts completed successfully but late.
- Overrun duration (t_1) as the lateness of completions with respect to bid durations.

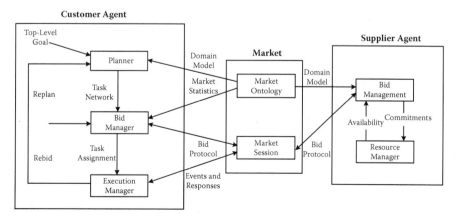

FIGURE 4.2 Overview of the Magnet system. (Adapted from Collins, J., C. Bilot, M. Gini, and B. Mobasher. 2001. *IEEE Internet Computing* 5(2): 61–72. With permission.)

For each of these factors, the market maintains the sample mean, the sample size, and the variance so that the agents can compute a confidence interval and present a risk report to the user.

The following formula is used to estimate risk (R). It is the absolute value of the negative part of the expected value computation:

$$R = \left| \sum_{i=1}^{n} \left(-z_i(1 - p_i) \prod_{j=1}^{i-1} p_j \right) \right| \qquad (4.2)$$

where z_i is the cumulative debit result from each completed task, and p_i is the success probability of the tasks. The customer agent can use risk data during the bidding cycle and during the bid evaluation.

4.2.4   SIZE ESTIMATION BY EVANS ET AL.

In the area of multiagent architectures for scalable high-performance networks, Evans et al. (1999) introduces the *total number of links* within a network. In a simplified network structure, the connection to the neighbors is managed by a hybrid authority. To manage the communication in the network, it is necessary to measure the total number of communication links to prevent overload conditions. In the example, each network region is managed by a central authority switch with eight neighbors. The size of each region is defined by its radius m, so that the number of switches in each region is $(2m + 1)^2$. The size of each network is defined by its radius n, so that the number of regions is $(2n + 1)^2$. The *total number of links* in the network is as follows:

$$N_L = 2\big((2m+1)(2n+1)-1\big)\big(2(2m+1)(2n+1)-1\big) \qquad (4.3)$$

With the special conditions of regional boundaries, the *total number of links* contained in a region is as follows:

$$N_{L\ in} = 4m(4m+1)(2n+1)^2 \qquad (4.4)$$

In a distributed MAS, these values can be used to split the network into regions to minimize the mean reroute response time. Evans et al. show that the scalability improves dramatically in a hybrid architecture if the number of regions is increased.

4.2.5   LOAD MANAGEMENT BY GUSTAVSSON

A simulation of an auction for load management based on utility agents, service agents, and device agents (HomeBots) for electric energy regulation is described in Gustavsson (1999). The modeled load balancing system is based on an MAS and allows for the design and implementation of highly efficient distributed auction algorithms. Gustavsson describes the following evaluation criteria for the system:

- *Scale* means that thousands or millions of devices can be handled simultaneously by the market mechanism.
- *Flexibility* based on local information and intelligence by agents includes more flexibility than a single point of control that has to know and steer everything.
- *Adaptability* means that the environment of the system changes dynamically with loads entering or disappearing at unknown and irregular times.
- *Customizability* means that the model gives room for individual customer requirements.
- *Wide Applicability* means that the given example for load management can be adapted in many different applications and scenarios.

In the simulations, they tested different algorithms by changing the use of power and measuring the time as the number of auction rounds needed to reach the goal that the market process is complete and no agent wants to buy or sell energy.

4.2.6 COALITION EVALUATION BY KATOH ET AL.

An MAS based on a loose coalition is shown in Katoh, Kinoshita, and Shiratori (2000), which presents cooperation relations among agents by a function of subjective information of an agent about another. This function defines a threshold at which to evaluate agents whether they cooperate or not. The measurement of this coalition considers dynamic properties such as *reliability, ability,* and *busyness* and is related to *agent performance.*

An example of how the subjects and the attributes of the subjective information can be used looks like: (agent B, Reliability, 10)$_A$. That means that agent A has the subjective information regarding the *reliability* of agent B and the current value is 10.

To evaluate the loose coalition, Katoh has performed some experiments. The starting point was a set of user agents and task agents. At the initial state, there is no loose coalition between the agents. The following values are measured:

- Number of successful tasks
- Average success rates
- Number of proceeded subtasks
- Processing time per subtask

Making tests with 500 and 5000 tasks by comparing different systems, they get information about the MAS performance. Measuring the average number of members of the loose coalition over a time frame shows when the loose coalition of agents has reached an optimum. As a result, it is important to propagate information of agents with higher reliability as soon as possible to design efficient MASs based on loose coalition.

4.2.7 COORDINATION EVALUATION BY TOLKSDORF

Software systems like MASs become more and more fine grained. Issues on interaction and coordination among the agents in such a system grow in importance. Based on a review of several coordination models from various disciplines, Tolksdorf (2000) describes how a reference model can look. The order scale of the evaluation of the coordination is based on the following characteristics:

- *Clear distinction* among interactors, noninteractors, and management relations.
- *Orthogonality* of the coordination model with computational models.
- Degree of *coupling* between interactors.
- Degree of *autonomy* of interactors.
- Management of relations is *external* or not.
- Amount of *awareness* required to manage the interactions.
- Degree of *stability of interactors.*
- *Stability of relations* assumed by the model.
- Assumed *reliability* about the interactors.
- *Scalability* provided by the model.
- *Usability* of the model for programming coordination.
- Qualitative or quantitative *measures* on the provided management of relations.

During the review of the different coordination models, Tolksdorf outlined a table-based overview. Under qualitative and quantitative measurement aspects the models have the results shown in Table 4.2.

Only the workflow management system and the formal models provide core measures of how optimally a situation is coordinated. On the other hand, these models are more static, centralized, and not as scalable.

4.2.8 THE SIMPLE THREAD LANGUAGE (STL)-BASED SIMULATION BY SCHUMACHER

Based on an improved Simple Thread Language (STL++), a simulation model is described in Schumacher (2001) that supports the development of an MAS as collective robots. In the simulation, different init agents encapsulate and handle their subenvironment as a part of the simulation environment. These parts of the environment, called *blub*, are under the control of the init agents, and they have to create other agents, handling the communication and so on. The agents in the MAS simulate robots that have sensors and can act in their subenvironment. To manage the subenvironment, the init agents have to measure the following aspects within every subenvironment:

- The size of the cell.
- The number of agents in the cell.
- The position of the agents in the cell.

TABLE 4.2

Measurement Intentions in Coordination Models

Model	Naive	Mintzberg	Coord	Formal	DAI/MAS	Linda	WfMC
Result	No	No	No	Yes	No	No	Yes

Over special ports, taxi agents are able to migrate from one subenvironment to another subenvironment. To analyze the experiment, every result is collected during the entire experiment.

4.2.9 MAS INFORMATION MODEL SIMULATION BY EGASHIRA AND HASHIMOTO

Based on an information model in an MAS, the different effects of information handling in a social order supported by common norms and social implications is considered in Egashira and Hashimoto (2001). The model deals with the role of social norms, when information is transferred between agents. Considering the role or function of social institutions, it is important to take into account the individual interpretation of information while social institutions emerge from the interaction of individuals. The model is used to analyze problems that emerge in the process of forming communication frameworks between individuals. When two agents communicate with each other, they have to receive and understand the information. It is clear that it is difficult for agent communication to be successful when a sender and a receiver interpret the information by using their own subjective frameworks. In a set of simulations, special filters for the information senders and receivers were used. The following values are measured to confirm the model:

- The time evolution of the number of clients.
- The dynamics of the number of clients.
- Transition of averaged score.
- The average number of clients of the sender.

The model shows that establishing norms facilitates the transfer of information, but it is sometimes distributed by a different type of norm organized through interaction between receivers. In the model, the correctness of the information cannot be directly checked by the agent. The basis for checking the correctness is the relationship between senders and receivers. In this sense, the reliability of information is represented by a norm that develops between senders and receivers. The simulation shows from which factors this norm derives.

4.2.10 ANALYSIS OF AGENT POPULATIONS BY LIU

In the area of self-organized intelligence in an MAS, Liu (2001) introduced two examples. One example is an agent system for searching and tracking digital image features, and another one is for controlling a group of distributed robots to navigate in an unknown task environment. The goal of the work is to empirically investigate the performance of agent behavior, self-organization incorporating local memory driven behavioral selection, and global performance driven behavioral learning with respect to goal attainability as well as task efficiency of the MAS. According to the adaptation facilities of the MAS, the development of the population of the active agents is investigated. Autonomous agents, whose age does not exceed a given life span, should evaluate the pixel gray level intensity by analyzing the images. When the agent in the location (i, j) is centered in a given location with radius $R(i, j)$ and detects feature pixels, then the MAS will reproduce a finite number of offspring agents. The trigger function to measure the pixel density distribution can be defined as follows:

$$D_{m(i,j)}^{R} = \sum_{s=-R}^{R} \sum_{t=-R}^{r} \left\{ s^0 t^0 \left\| m(i+s, j+t) - m(i, j) \right\| < \delta \right\} \tag{4.5}$$

where R is the radius of a circular region centered at (i, j); s, t are the indices of the neighboring pixel relative to (i, j); $m(i, j)$ is the gray level at the location (i, j); and δ is a predefined positive constant.

In examples, Liu shows that the self-reproducing agents can be used to quickly figure out moving targets in a dynamic multiagent environment.

4.2.11 BUSINESS-TO-BUSINESS (B2B) MODEL PERFORMANCE BY OUKSEL ET AL.

The effectiveness and efficiency of business-to-business agents in an MAS e-commerce environment is described in Ouksel, Babad, and Tesch (2004). They analyzed matchmaking in a stable two-sided market, where each seller is matched with a single buyer, and all agents on both sides are matched. To measure the performance of the model, a two-agents system has been used consecutively. At each time stamp t, there is a set of alternatives A_t for which the first agent (called agent U) has utilities U_t, and the second (called agent V) has utilities V_t. The agents report to the arbiter the utilities u_t and v_t, which are subsets of U_t and V_t. In this case, the agents are honest, $U_t = u_t$ and $V_t = v_t$, but in general, they may hide or falsify some of their utilities. Using the model, the gain of agent U at the conclusion of trade at time stamp t is as follows:

$$gain_t(U) = U_t \big(f(u_t, v_t) \big), \tag{4.6}$$

and similarly for agent V. Over a sequence of m trades, the average gain of agent U is as follows:

$$avggain_m(U) = \left[\sum_t gain_t(U) \right] / m, \tag{4.7}$$

and similarly for agent V.

The used measure for the performance of the model by Ouksel is defined as:

$$neteff_m = \left[avggain_m(U) + avggain_m(V) \right] / 2 \tag{4.8}$$

The performance measure for the model allows for the comparison of different trading protocols like deterministic compensational arbitration, Nash protocol, and maximal sum protocol. The analysis of this performance shows a significant increase of net efficiency with matchmaking, particularly for the probabilistic protocol.

4.2.12 PERFORMANCE MEASUREMENT OF LARGE DISTRIBUTED MAS BY HELSINGER

An example of performance measurement of a large distributed MAS is given in Helsinger et al. (2003). Helsinger describes the tools, techniques, and results of performance characterization of the Cougaar distributed agent architecture. The starting point is an overview about difficulties in measuring the performance of an MAS, and the following points are presented:

- Difficulty of voluminous data generated by the MAS.
- Difficulty of coordination data gathering and retrieval.
- Difficulty of measurement impact performance.
- Difficulty of changing needs and priorities during lifetime.
- Difficulty of performance measurement requirements needs for measuring an MAS.

Helsinger categorizes the use of performance measurement data in different ways. A first way is given by the answer to the question, "Who uses the data?". A second categorization is given by the intended use of the data. Third, Helsinger classifies metrics data based on the method used for their propagation. The last categorization is based on the different abstraction levels for MAS performance metrics. Figure 4.3 will give an overview about these methods of categorization.

The presented Cougaar agent architecture for building large distributed MASs is based on Java and includes around 400,000 lines of code. The system includes several subsystems for measuring performance data. Application metrics like network, CPU, and memory usage statistics can be used to manage and to examine the application at run-time. The agent architecture level instrumentation captures data intrinsic to the MAS architecture. The metrics can be used by an internal adaptation engine to optimize system performance and by an external system designer to evaluate the architecture performance. The feature to provide the metric service in the Cougaar architecture is called agent blackboard. The blackboard metrics service provides a set of performance metrics to applications and infrastructure components. Table 4.3 presents a list of metrics available from the blackboard service.

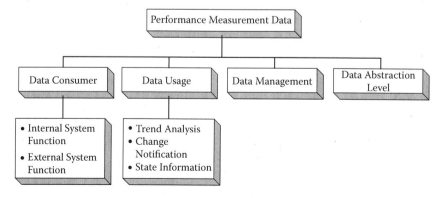

FIGURE 4.3   Categorization approach for performance measurement data.

TABLE 4.3
Cougaar Blackboard Metrics

Metric	Description
Asset count	The total number of "asset" objects on the local blackboard
Plan element count	The total number of "plan element" objects on the local blackboard
Task count	Count of "tasks" on the local blackboard
Object count	Count of objects on the local blackboard
Custom object count	Count objects matching a user-specified predicate

TABLE 4.4
Message Transport Metrics

Metric	Description
Queue length	The average number of outgoing messages waiting to be sent
Message bytes	The total size of all messages
Message count	The number of sent messages

The message transport service captures statistics about the messages that flow through it. These statistics can be used for real-time adaptation as well as trend analysis. An overview about the metrics available from the message transport service is given in Table 4.4.

The Cougaar architecture includes a number of plug-ins for the purpose of metrics collections. Additionally, an event logging service allows process logging, and customer servlets provide an out-of-band data access mechanism for Cougaar agents.

4.2.13 Measurement of Coordination Performance by Ahn and Park

The evaluation of an MAS for distributed coordination (MADC) is presented by Ahn and Park (2003). The performance of MADC was analyzed by simulation experiments. To compare different strategies of the MADC under performance aspects, the two measures *inventory level* and *service rate* are used. Service rate is defined as the proportion of buyers' orders that are fulfilled by suppliers. A service rate like 0.9 means that in a special time unit 100 products are ordered and 90 products are actually delivered.

4.2.14 Performance Measurement in Telematics by Gerber

Other examples for MAS performance measurement are given in Gerber (2001). The Mobility and Transport in Inter-modular Traffic (MoTiV-PTA) project has the goal to develop a unified distributed telematics system for planning and supporting individual intermodal travel. Before the system can be introduced into the marketplace, a series of test runs and simulations based on a multiagent simulation framework are used. The current processing speed *currentSpeed* ∈ [0;400] depends on the number of agents running on the server and the maximal speed of the server:

$$currentSpeed = maxSpeed \times min\left(1, \frac{5}{numberOfChannels}\right) \quad (4.9)$$

with *maxSpeed* ∈ [0;400] and *numberOfChannels* ∈ [0;50].

Later, Gerber describes the performance of measurement-based self-adaptation of the MAS-based information system. The Java-based MAS is located on a variable number of servers, and to obtain the fundamentals for self-adaptation, they measure the server performance. The performance of every server is given by the *number of communication acts of logged agents per minute*. Overall performance is measured by averaging the *duration time of a representative variety of servers over a time period*. To perform an optimization step, the performance measurement based workload of the agent servers is used.

The result can be to put up a new server, if required, or shut down a server if possible. The certain factor a_i is used to find a position for a new server close to servers with a more than average number of agents and a less than average performance:

$$a_i = min\left(1, \frac{performance_i}{performance_{avg}} \times \frac{AgentList_i}{AgentList_{avg}}\right) \quad (4.10)$$

4.2.15 PERFORMANCE MEASUREMENT IN TELECOMMUNICATION BY GIBNEY ET AL.

Gibney et al. (2001) present an example of the performance evaluation of an MAS for market-based call routing in telecommunication networks. The experimental evaluation is designed to find an answer for the following two fundamental questions: Can the market-based control system perform as well or better than a conventional system? Is the effect of using a Vickrey auction protocol rather than a first-price auction protocol at the path market? In a series of experiments, they test the efficiency of the marked-based control mechanism. The experiment runs as a simulation in a small, irregular network of 8 nodes with link capacities for 200 channels over a defined time. As a metric for the performance, they use the proportion of calls successfuly routed through the network as a percentage of the total number of calls.

4.2.16 ALGORITHM PERFORMANCE MEASUREMENT BY PATEL ET AL.

Also, Patel, Barria, and Pitt (2001) use a performance measure to evaluate different algorithms for market-based MAS in telecommunication systems. Different algorithms, such as resource-oriented and price-oriented algorithms, are compared with the focus on their ability to effectively control the traffic load. In simulations, they test the different algorithms with a controlled traffic load of 35%, 90%, and 150% of system capacity. As a result, the price-oriented algorithm performs in the range of the simulation better than the resource-oriented algorithm.

4.2.17 Performance Measurement Approach by Stojanov et al.

Another example of an implicit MAS measurement is given by Stojanov et al. (2000), considering the MAS performance by describing a protocol of agent interaction in an MAS related to two measurement points, as can be seen in Figure 4.4. The result allows us to consider the performance of the different orthogonal function realizations.

Based on the MALINA model, some agent-oriented metrics are given in Stojanov (2004). The agent-oriented metrics are categorized in three groups:

1. Basic metrics
2. Introspective metrics
3. External metrics

A possible model for the automated control of measurement and evaluation in MALINA is based on two components:

1. *Meta Model*: A specification of the metric classification.
2. *Metric Models*: As the description of the concrete metrics.

To integrate the measurement model in MALINA, it will be implemented as a run-time module.

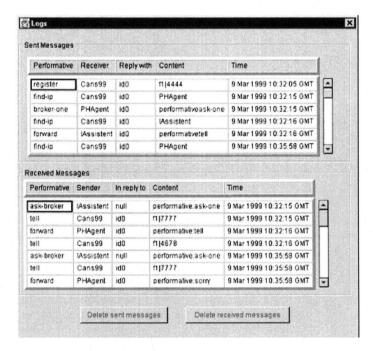

FIGURE 4.4   Performance measurement of agent interaction in MALINA.

4.2.18   Quality Evaluation of an MAS by Far

The quality of MASs as software systems can be characterized with terms like "conformance to requirements" or "fitness for use." A good-quality MAS should include fewer bugs and provide better user satisfaction. The quality criteria *usability, functionality, performance, reliability, installability, maintainability, documentation, availability, efficiency,* and *portability* for an MAS can be found in Far (2002). To evaluate the quality of an MAS, these criteria have to be mapped to measurable metrics.

As examples, Far introduces two kinds of complexity metrics for an MAS. The subjective complexity metrics can be used when a human user evaluates the complexity of the system. A modified version of function point (*FP*) can be used to account for the algorithmic complexity. For every agent in the MAS, the following parameters are involved: external inputs (N_i), external outputs (N_o), external inquiries (N_q), external interfaces (N_{ef}), internal data structures (N_{if}), algorithmic complexity (N_m), and knowledge complexity factor (N_k). The algorithmic complexity (N_m) factor is the sum of three Boolean variables stating whether cooperative, coordinative, and competitive mechanisms are implemented or not ($0 \le N_m \le 3$). The knowledge complexity factor (N_k) is a value between 0 and 5 depending whether the agent has a knowledge-base and whether the knowledge-base is sharable or is based on a shared ontology. The unweighted function points (UF_eC) are as follows:

$$UF_eC = 4N_i + 5N_o + 4N_q + 7N_{ef} + 7N_{if} + 10N_m + 6N_k \tag{4.11}$$

The adjusted MAS function point (*MAS FP*) will be derived by multiplying UF_eC with the subjective assessment of technical complexity.

As an objective metric, the objective complexity as an internal property of the MAS is presented. If the MAS system is nearly decomposable, the cyclomatic complexity metrics can be used. The complexity of the MAS is the sum of the cyclomatic complexities of the constituent agents. As a measure for nearly decomposable, the communicative cohesion metrics can be examined. The communicative cohesion metric (*CMM*) for an agent g_i is defined in terms of the ratio of internal relationships (interactions) to the total number of relationships (sum of interactions and intra-actions):

$$CMM(g_i) = \frac{R_{internal}}{R_{internal} + R_{external}} \tag{4.12}$$

The CMM for the MAS is the statistical mean of CMM of its constituent agents. Systems with CMM $\ge$ 0.91 are usually considered to be nearly decomposable.

4.2.19   Scalability of an MAS by Rana and Stout

Scalability as the ability of a solution to a problem to work when the size of the problem increases is presented from the view of the MAS presented by Rana and Stout

(2000). Outgoing from a performance engineering perspective, Rana introduces the following needs to scale for an MAS:

- When the total number of agents involved increases on a given platform.
- When the total number of agents involved increases across multiple systems or platforms.
- When the size of the data that the agents are processing increases.
- When the diversity of agents increases.

The following are ideas for scalability measurement. The total agent density and the resulting effect on system performance can be determined in terms of metrics associated with a particular platform or an operating environment. These metrics include *memory usage, scheduling/swapping overheads, cloning agents,* or *dispatching an agent* to a remote side, and they are often the only metrics reported for agent performance and scalability. The *relative speed up* can be measured if agent density is increased to obtain a better performance. These metrics can be used to manage an increasing number of agents.

Scalability of an MAS can also be stated in terms of *coordination policies* in the agent community and in terms of the *total number of messages* that are necessary to be exchanged to converge on a solution.

To identify metrics for measuring scalability of an MAS, Rana proposes two categories of metrics. The first category is related to system parameters and the second to coordination mechanisms. The system metrics are generally measured as time parameters in the following manner:

- Start an agent, which would involve loading and running a class file (Java). This will also include setup time to listen on a port for incoming messages from other agents.
- Deactivate/activate an agent where persistence mechanisms are supported. This would involve checkpointing an agent and storing its current state.
- Schedule an agent activity on the host.
- In the case of mobile agents, the time to receive and buffer incoming agents and register them with local stationary agents.

The times for single agents can be summed up over all agents and weighted.

As scalability metrics for the coordination category, Rana presents the following metrics:

- The total number of messages transferred between agents.
- Time to reach an agreement between agents.
- Total number of involved agents.
- The maximal distance between involved agents.
- The number of agents involved in subgroups.
- The total number of simultaneously supported conversations.
- The response time between conversations.

From the viewpoint of collaboration on scaling the MAS, the following metrics can be used:

- Number of links between agents.
- Required time for sending messages between agents.
- Time to perform computation at each agent.

Based on these metrics, an introduction to a framework for modeling agent communities under scalability aspects with Petri nets is given. The model is demonstrated with an e-commerce-based application, consisting of two buyer agents, two seller agents, and one facilitator agent running on different hosts.

4.2.20   Performance Measurement by Cortese et al.

Another measurement approach for scalability and performance measurement is given in Cortese et al. (2003). He introduces the scalability and performance of the JAVA Agent Development Framework (JADE) MAS message transport system. The following agent platform characteristics for the evaluation of the agent system are presented:

- Interoperability
- Cost and maintainability of the code
- Memory requirements
- Messaging performance

Test-bed-based measurement of the round-trip time, as the required time for a circular exchange of agent communication language (ACL) messages between the sender agent and the receiver agent, is presented. To evaluate the scalability of the platform, the starting point is a single couple of sender/receiver. By increasing the number of couples, it can be observed how the round-trip time is affected. For each measurement, the round-trip time for message exchanges of each couple and the number of couples are collected.

Tests have been arranged for the following:

- Interplatform communication, where the agents are on different platforms running on different hosts.
- Intraplatform communications, where the agents are in two containers on two similar hosts.
- Intraplatform communication offered by JADE middleware.
- Communication based on Requirements Modeling Language (RML) implementation.

Using a reference hardware for all tests, the measurement results can be used to compare the tests. Globally, the result was that JADE is a good candidate for heavy-loaded distributed application because it scales linearly with the load conditions.

4.2.21　A METRIC FOR TRUST IN AGENT COMMUNITIES BY WENG ET AL.

Weng et al. (2006) show that a trust-based community outperforms a similarly based item recommendation system in terms of prediction accuracy, coverage, and robustness. Therefore, they present a metric, calculating the trustworthiness of an agent s in agent t:

$$Tr_{s,t} = \frac{N \sum_i \sum_j \frac{n_{ij}^2}{C_j} - \sum_i R_j^2}{N^2 - \sum_i R_i^2} \tag{4.13}$$

In this metric, N determines the number of items that are co-rated by both agents; the other variables are related to the agent's opinions and co-rated items. They are stored and updated within a data structure as shown in Table 4.5.

4.2.22　BENCHMARK-BASED MAS EVALUATION BY ZHANG ET AL.

An approach for the evaluation of an MAS's performance by a benchmark-based framework is described in Zhang, Wallis, and Johnston (2005). With the example of supply chain management, the authors prove the performance gain in real-world applications of distributed agent intelligence. Thereby, the overall goal is implemented within the single agent behaviors. The temporal variables t_k and t_s are chosen to measure the interruption of behaviors as the waiting time and, respectively, the idling time. The agents measure the values and any transgression about preset limits $[T_k, T_s]$ that triggers an adjustment process.

TABLE 4.5
Agent s Experience with Agent t

Agent s Opinions	Agent t Opinions					Total
	1	...	j	...	Z	
1	n_{11}	...	n_{1j}	...	n_{1Z}	R_1
$\vdots$	$\vdots$		$\vdots$		$\vdots$	$\vdots$
i	n_{i1}	...	n_{ij}	...	n_{iZ}	R_i
$\vdots$	$\vdots$		$\vdots$		$\vdots$	$\vdots$
Z	n_{Z1}	...	n_{Zj}	...	n_{ZZ}	R_Z
Total	C_1	...	C_j	...	C_Z	N

The presented performance results based on simulations are as follows:

- Greater demand variation is easier to handle with agent technology
- Easier stock handling with agents
- Reduced back orders

The authors present a framework that incorporates the association of system goals with agent behaviors, thereby simplifying MAS design through reduction of burden and communication costs.

4.3 DISCUSSION

The summary of the inventory of shown quality measurement approaches in the area of MASs is presented in Figure 4.5.

Most criteria are similar to the inventory of software agent measurement intentions. Figure 4.5 shows that most examples are about performance and communication. Other criteria with high agent technology relevance, like cooperation and intelligence, have been presented in only a few investigations.

Without performance and communication, measurement plays only a very small role in MASs. For many criteria, such as security, maintainability, functionality, and trustworthiness, no quality measurement examples can be found.

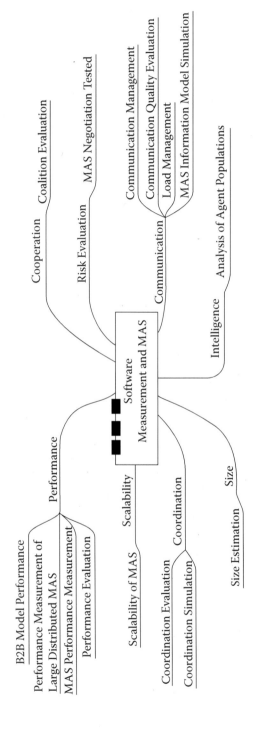

FIGURE 4.5   General overview about the use of measurement in the area of multiagent systems.

REFERENCES

Ahn, H. J. and S. J. Park. 2003. Modeling of a Multi-Agent System for Coordination of Supply Chains with Complexity and Uncertainty. In *Intelligent Agents and Multi-Agent Systems 6th Pacific Rim International Workshop on Multi-Agents (PRIMA 2003),* ed. J. Lee and M. Barley, 13–24. Berlin: Springer.

Collins, J., C. Bilot, M. Gini, and B. Mobasher. 2001. Decision Processes in Agent-Based Automated Contracting. *IEEE Internet Computing* 5(2): 61–72.

Cortese, E., F. Quarta, G. Vitaglione, and P. Vrba. 2003. Scalability and Performance of the JADE Message Transport System. In *Proceedings of the International Conference on Autonomous Agents,* 52–65. New York: ACM Press.

Egashira, S. and T. Hashimoto. 2001. The Formation of Common Norms on the Assumption of "Fundamentally" Imperfect Information. In *Social Order in Multiagent Systems,* ed. R. Conte and C. Dellarocas, 181–198. Boston: Kluwer Academic.

Evans, R., F. Sommers, D. Kerr, and D. O'Sullivan. 1999. A Multi-Agent System Architecture for Scalable Management of High Performance Networks: Applying Arms Length Autonomy. In *Software Agents for Future Communication Systems,* ed. A. L. G. Hayzelden and J. Bigham, 86–111. Berlin: Springer.

Far, B. H. 2002. Software Agents: Quality, Complexity and Uncertainty Issues. In *Proceedings of the 1st IEEE International Conference on Cognitive Informatics,* ed. T. Wang and M. R. Smith, 122–131. Los Altimos, CA: IEEE Computer Society Press.

Gerber, C. 2001. Self-Adaptation for Performance Optimisation in an Agent-Based Information System. In *Agent Technology for Communication Infrastructures,* ed. A. L. G. Hayzelden and R. A. Bourne, 122–143. Chichester: John Wiley & Sons.

Gibney, M. A., N. R. Jennings, N. J. Vriend, and J. M. Griffiths. 2001. Market-Based Call Routing in Telecommunications Networks Using Adaptive Pricing and Real Bidding. In *Agent Technology for Communication Infrastructures,* ed. A. L. G. Hayzelden and R. A. Bourne, 234–248. Chichester: John Wiley & Sons.

Gustavsson, R. 1999. Agents with Power. *Communications of the ACM* 42(3): 41–47.

Helsinger, A., R. Lazarus, W. Wright, and J. Zinky. 2003. Tools and Techniques for Performance Measurement of Large Distributed Multiagent Systems. In *Proceedings of the Second International Joint Conference on Autonomous Agents and Multiagent Systems,* 843–850. Los Altimos, CA: IEEE Computer Society Press.

Katoh, T., T. Kinoshita, and N. Shiratori. 2000. Dynamic Properties of Multiagent Based on a Mechanism of Loose Coalition. In *Design and Applications of Intelligent Agents,* Lecture Notes in Artificial Intelligence 1881, ed. C. Zhang, and V. W. Soo, 16–30. Berlin: Springer.

Liu, J. 2001. Self-Organized Intelligence. In *Agent Engineering,* ed. J. Liu, N. Zhong, Y. Y. Tang, and P. S. P. Wang, 123–148. Singapore: World Scientific.

Lukschandl, E. 2001. Evolving Routing Algorithms with Genetic Programming. In *Agent Technology for Communication Infrastructures,* ed. A. L. G. Hayzelden and R. A. Bourne, 287–294. Chichester: John Wiley & Sons.

Ouksel, A., Y. M. Babad, and T. Tesch. 2004. Matchmaking Software Agents in B2B Markets. In *Proceedings of the 37th Annual Hawaii International Conference on System Sciences (HICSS'04),* Track 7. Los Altimos, CA: IEEE Computer Society Press.

Patel, A., J. Barria, and J. Pitt. 2001. IN Load Control Algorithms for Market-Based Multi-Agent Systems. In *Agent Technology for Communication Infrastructures,* ed. A. L. G. Hayzelden, and R. A. Bourne, 249–265. Chichester: John Wiley & Sons.

Pham, H. H. 2002. Software Agents for Internet-Based System and Their Design. In *Intelligent Agents and Their Applications,* ed. L. C. Jain, Z. Chen, and N. Ichalkaranje, 101–147. Heidelberg: Physica.

Rana, O. F. and K. Stout. 2000. What Is Scalability in Multi-Agent Systems? In *Proceedings of the 4th International Conference on Autonomous Agents*, ed. R. Feiertag, J. Rho, and S. Rosset, 53–63. Barcelona, Spain: IEEE Computer Society Press.

Schumacher, M. 2001. *Objective Coordination in Multi-Agent System Engineering.* Berlin: Springer.

Stojanov, S. 2004. *MALINA — An Agent-Oriented Development Tool Environment* (German). In *Proceedings of the 5th Workshop Performance Engineering in Software Development at Siemens Munich (PE 2004)*, ed. A. Schmietendorf and R. Dumke, 95–104. Magdeburg: University Press.

Stojanov, S., M. Kumurdjieva, E. Dimitrov, and A. Schmietendorf. 2000. Technological Framework for Development of Agent-Based Applications. In *Proceedings of the Workshop Concurrency, Specification & Programming*, 299–311. Los Altimos, CA: IEEE Computer Society Press.

Tolksdorf, R. 2000. Models of Coordination. In *Engineering Societies in the Agent World*, Lecture Notes in Artificial Intelligence 1972, ed. A. Omincini, R. Tolksdorf, and F. Zambonelli, 78–92. Berlin: Springer

Weng, J., C. Miao, A. Goh, Z. Shen, and R. Gay. 2006. Trust-Based Agent Community for Collaborative Recommendation. In *Proceedings of the 5th International Joint Conference on Autonomous Agents Multiagent Systems (AAMAS 2006)*, 1260–1262. Los Altimos, CA: IEEE Computer Society Press.

Zhang, J., P. Wallis, and R. B. Johnston. 2005. Intelligent Kanban: Evaluation of a Supply Chain MAS Application Using Benchmarking. In *The 2005 IEEE International Conference on e-Technology, e-Commerce and e-Service (EEE 2005)*, ed. J. Stouby et al., 396–399. Los Altimos, CA: IEEE Computer Society Press.

5 Quality-Based Development of Agent Systems

5.1 INTRODUCTION

How software quality measurement is included in the process of agent-based system development will be analyzed in this chapter (Figure 5.1). It has been shown that a lot of different multiagent systems (MASs) exist, and every year new ones will be developed. A review of available sources should help us to get an overview about what is missing now.

Jennings and Wooldridge defined the following bottleneck in 1998, and we want to illustrate how the situation is now:

> There is little in the way of production-quality software support for building agent applications, and still less general understanding of the issues that need to be addressed when building such systems. Worse, most of today's agent systems are built from scratch, using bespoke tools and techniques, which cannot easily be applied to other types of systems. This is particularly worrying because a lot of infrastructure is required before the main components of an agent system can be built. At the moment, most developers rebuild this infrastructure from scratch in every new case; this process is clearly not sustainable. (p. 19)

The development of an MAS includes in a general sense all phases of the traditional software development process. These phases are problem definition, requirements analysis, specification, design, implementation, test, and supply (Dumke 2003). This chapter gives a summary of our review of existing quality measurement intentions in this area.

5.2 QUALITY MEASUREMENT EXAMPLES OF MULTIAGENT SYSTEM (MAS) DEVELOPMENT

5.2.1 ASPECT-ORIENTED VERSUS PATTERN-ORIENTED MAS DEVELOPMENT BY GARCIA ET AL.

One example given in Garcia, Lucena, and Cowan (2004) is a validation of two different MAS development methods. A qualitative and quantitative study compares the aspect-oriented development method with a pattern-oriented development method. Two teams designed and implemented the MASs for portalware agents based on the

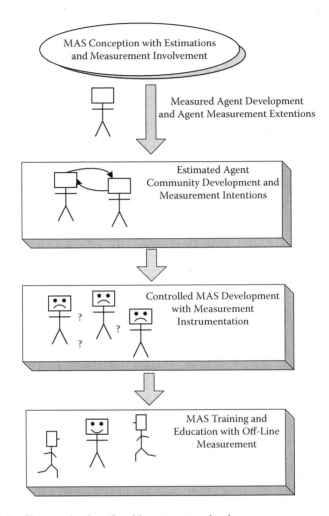

FIGURE 5.1   Characterization of multiagent system development.

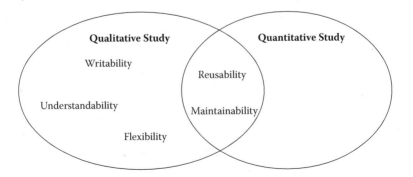

FIGURE 5.2   Quality criteria to evaluate portalware multiagent systems.

TABLE 5.1

Association between Metrics, Goal Question Metric (GQM) Questions and Principles

Metrics	Answered Questions	Principles
Vocabulary Size (VS)	How many components (classes/aspects) are in the design?	Size
Lines of Code (LOC)	How many lines of code are there in the implementation?	Size
Number of Attributes (NOA)	How many attributes are there in the components?	Size
Weighted Methods per Component (WMC)	How many operations (methods/advices) are there?	Size
Coupling Between Components (CBC)	How high is the coupling between components?	Coupling
Lack of Cohesion in Methods (LOCM)	How high is the cohesion of the system components?	Cohesion
Depth of Inheritance Tree (DIT)	How high is the coupling between components? How high is the cohesion of the system components?	Coupling and cohesion
Concern Diffusion over Components (CDC)	How well are the agency concerns localized in terms of components?	Separation of concerns
Concern Diffusion over Operations (CDO)	How well are the agency concerns localized in terms of operations?	Separation of concerns
Concern Diffusion over LOC (CDLOC)	How well are the agency concerns localized in terms of LOC?	Separation of concerns

different methods. The qualitative study uses the criteria to evaluate the two methods shown in Figure 5.2.

The second part of the MAS evaluation as a quantitative study focuses on the criteria *maintenance* and *reuse*. Based on Basili's Goal Question Metric (GQM) methodology, Garcia identified useful software metrics. The relationships of metrics to the main questions and selected principles are shown in Table 5.1.

The quality model breaks down the relationship between the metrics, principles, factors, and qualities. The high-level quality criteria maintainability and reusability are mapped to quality factors and then to traditional software engineering principles. Each principle is associated with a metric set based on the GQM methodology (Figure 5.3).

Evaluation of the aspect-oriented and pattern-oriented developed MAS shows that the analyzed and measured criteria are useful for the qualitative and quantitative study. Garcia shows that in most cases the aspect-oriented MASs perform better. When analyzing the results of these studies, the following measurement aspects can be identified as important:

- The qualitative comparison of writability, reusability, maintainability, and flexibility produces significant differences between the MAS development methods.

- All separation-of-concerns metrics provide good support for the separation of MASs.
- All size metrics produce good results in the sense of how concise the MASs are.
- The metric *coupling between components* (CBC) produces significant results during the comparison.
- The metric *depth of inheritance tree* detects a problem to the abuse of the inheritance mechanism by one of the MAS development methods.
- The metric *lack of cohesion in methods* shows a problem in encapsulated behaviors that act over different components.

5.2.2 EVALUATION OF MAS BASED ON THE ROADMAP META-MODEL BY JUAN AND STERLING

The ROADMAP meta-model (Juan and Sterling 2003, 2004; Juan, Sterling, and Winikoff 2003) is a generic meta-model for describing and developing an MAS. The model presents a high-level abstract specification of requirements, capturing organizational structures, regulations, processes, goals, responsibilities, and various permissions for the agents to function in the MAS (Figure 5.4).

Juan and Sterling discuss new and imprecise quality attributes for MASs as non-functional requirements and "soft goals." They explain that traditional software

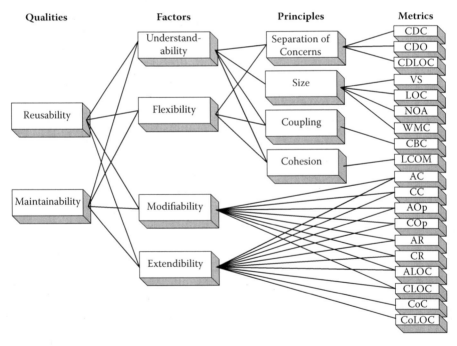

FIGURE 5.3 The quality model to evaluate a portalware MAS. (Adapted from Garcia, Lucena, and Cowan 2004.)

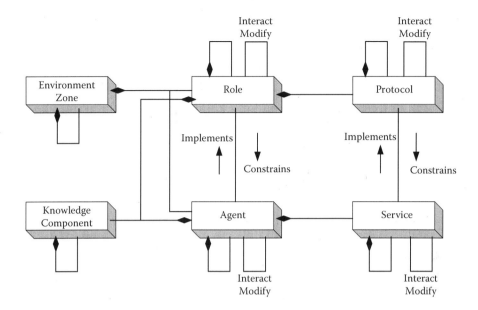

FIGURE 5.4 The ROADMAP meta-model.

quality attributes cannot guarantee that the correctness holds after deployment. In traditional software systems, the system will be tested before release against documented requirements. In an MAS, the system behavior changes due to continuous adaptation and the possibility of misbehaving new agents in the open environment. To solve this problem, they propose constructs to explicitly represent the correct system behavior and the required level of quality attributes to allow run-time validation of the system. As traditional quality attributes, they use *system performance, reliability, security, usability, and maintainability.* As new quality attributes, they explain *privacy, politeness, benevolence,* and *good taste.*

The meta-model should be used to ensure consistency between various MAS methodologies, computer-aided software engineering (CASE) tools, programming languages, and MAS frameworks. The evaluation of the ROADMAP meta-model based on eight criteria has the goal to guarantee that developed MASs fulfill quality requirements (Figure 5.5).

Evaluation of closeness to the object orientation (OO) approach considering the ROADMAP meta-model has the result that it fulfills the evaluation criteria well. No explicit measures are presented while only the criteria are discussed.

5.2.3 Agent Framework Evaluation by Tambe, Pynadath, and Chauvat

The evaluation of a framework for distributed and heterogeneous agents is presented by Tambe, Pynadath, and Chauvat (2000). The Karma-Teamcore framework focuses on enabling software developers to build large-scale agent organizations in cyberspace. Using the framework, the software developer interacts with the team-oriented programming interface (TOPI) to specify a team-oriented program

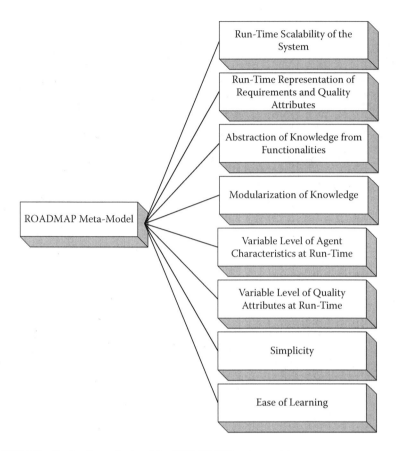

FIGURE 5.5   Evaluation criteria of the ROADMAP meta-model.

with an organization, goals, and plans. Karma derives the requirements for organizational roles and searches for agents with relevant expertise called domain agents. A central role in Karma plays the Teamcore wrapper that wraps an individual agent. All communication is based on Knowledge Query Manipulation Language (KQML), and the capabilities of the framework are established in the wrapper. To reach his goals, Karma uses middle agents as sources for searching. Karma is a Java-based agent that helps to build a team-oriented agent organization. To evaluate the Karma Teamcore framework, Tambe and colleagues describe the following aspects:

- Evaluating robustness as the fundamental motivation for the framework. If, for example, a Teamcore wrapper crashes another Teamcore wrapper that wraps, an agent with similar capabilities takes over.
- Evaluating wrapper benefits as a measure of Teamcore wrapper capabilities. To achieve this goal, they measure the number of messages exchanged over time in different runs. There were different runs with normal, cautious, and failed numbers of messages.

- Evaluating flexibility includes the aspect of how easy it is to make a modification of the team.

Tambe and colleagues illustrate that the Karma-based sets of heterogeneous distributed agents successfully execute the team-oriented program and in general are robust enough to survive as a team despite individual failures. To improve the robustness, future work in distributed monitoring is needed.

5.2.4 UNIFIED MODELING LANGUAGE (UML) AND MEASUREMENT INTENTIONS BY BERTOLINO, DIMITROV, DUMKE, AND LINDEMANN

For the evaluation of UML-based software or for evaluation of the UML development process, currently only modeling approaches and initial examples exist. The following measurement intentions are explained in Dumke (2003):

- Metrics for *class diagrams* are the number of stereotypes, persistent classes, abstract classes, the inheritance tree deepness, the parent classes, the child classes, and the operations and attributes of the class distinct after public, protected, and private.
- Metrics for *use case diagrams* are the number of abstract use cases, the reference to class diagrams, and the dependency of use cases from the actor.

For the process evaluation, metrics can be used as follows:

- Requirements evaluation.
- Consistency between the diagrams.
- Possibility to generate code from diagrams and reverse to generate diagrams from code.

As a resource evaluation metric, the CASE Tool efficiency from the view of a reduction of the development complexity can be used.

On the other hand, UML diagrams can be used to derivate measurement intentions. In the area of performance measurement, approaches are presented. Bertolino, Marchetti, and Mirandola (2002) describe the use of real-time UML for performance engineering. Another approach proposes extensions to UML state diagrams and activity diagrams to allow the association of events with exponentially distributed and deterministic delays (Lindemann et al. 2002). Using generalized semi-Markov processes (GSMPs), Figure 5.6 shows how to derivate performance measures out of UML diagrams.

This example outlines an idea to quantify performance measures out of UML diagrams. Checking the results against the UML diagrams, they can be used to evaluate the UML-based development process. The connection between UML and software measurement is really at the beginning, but the approaches will become even more important for agent and agent system development. In the future, UML-2.0-based timing diagrams as interaction diagrams showing the change in state or condition

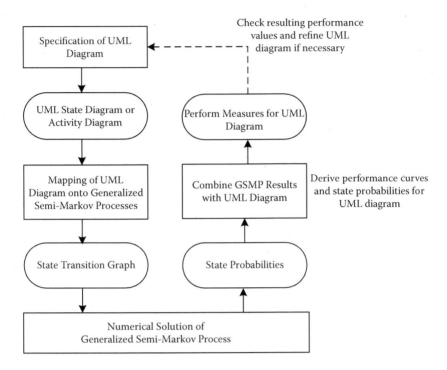

FIGURE 5.6 Derivation of quantitative performance measures out of Unified Modeling Language diagrams.

of a lifeline over linear time can be used to model performance-relevant parts of an agent system.

An extended overview about UML-based performance engineering possibilities and techniques can be found in Dimitrov, Schmietendorf, and Dumke (2002). Dimitrov characterizes three different UML-based approaches of performance engineering:

- The direct representation of performance aspects with UML diagrams.
- UML extensions that allow dealing with performance aspects.
- A combination of UML with techniques of formal description like Specification and Description Language (SDL) and Message Sequence Charts (MSCs).

The example of a sequence diagram presented in Figure 5.7 is a special kind of interaction diagram that offers the potential to obtain and present performance information.

Time attributes can be added to the messages at the horizontal lines and to the method execution at the vertical bars. The state marker in the sequence diagram offers the possibility to set up a reference between sequence and state diagrams. Unfortunately, the traditional UML tools do not support UML-based performance engineering aspects, and the UML-based approaches do not satisfy the early definition of performance requirements. Outgoing from a prototype-based case study for

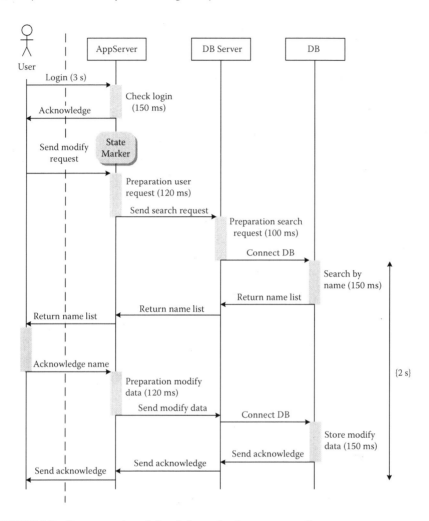

FIGURE 5.7   Representation of time information in a sequence diagram.

performance engineering with UML, Dimitrov defines the following proposal for an integrated approach:

- Extensions of UML notation to represent performance-related aspects.
- Waiting queue models or net-based models in the early stages.
- Tool-based solution techniques or formal description techniques in the late development stages.

5.2.5   AGENT COMMUNICATION LANGUAGE EVALUATION, SINGH

Some criteria to evaluate agent communication languages (ACLs) for an appropriate use are defined in Singh (1998). Based on analyzing existing ACLs, like Arcol and KQML, Singh examines the following elements to evaluate ACLs:

- *Perspective* as the potential of each communication for a sender, a receiver, and a society. Every communication in this sense has a private and public perspective.
- *Type of meaning* as three aspects of the formal study of a language like syntax, semantics, and pragmatics.
- *Context* as a general part to understand a communication in an agent's physical or simulated environment.
- *Coverage of communication acts* as the meaning of the exchanged information when heterogeneous and autonomous agents communicate. The seven categories are assertive, directive, commissive, permissive, prohibitive, declarative, and expressive.

From the view of agent construction, Singh describes the following elements for evaluation:

- *Mental versus social agency* as the relationship between the mental state of the agent as beliefs and intentions on one side, and the agents as social creatures in a social agency on the other side.
- *Design autonomy* as a minimization of requirements to promote heterogeneity as the freedom to have agents of different design and construction.
- *Execution autonomy* as the ability of an ACL to require agents to be sincere, cooperative, benevolent, and so on.

After answering questions about these criteria, the user can decide to use a specific ACL with respect to its limitations.

5.2.6 MULTIAGENT SYSTEM (MAS) DEVELOPMENT APPROACH EVALUATION BY LIND

In Lind (2001), there is a discussion of different approaches that were specifically built for the development of MAS. Together with a general view on the MAS, Lind defines properties to evaluate the MAS. The following properties are defined and used for a ranking:

- *Generality* is the range of an MAS that is supported or the commitment to a particular technology or agent architecture.
- *Flexibility* covers aspects such as the extensibility of the method or support for different process models or tools.
- *Granularity* captures the level of detail by which system aspects can be modeled and the supported levels of abstraction.
- *Formality* is the use of formal methods or well-defined semantics of modeling elements.
- *Tool support* summarizes available tools for a particular method.

TABLE 5.2

Evaluation of Chosen Multiagent System Development Methods

Method	Generality	Flexibility	Granularity	Formality	Tool Support
Burmeister	7	4	3	2	1
Kinny/ Georgeff	3	5	2	4	2
DESIRE	9	2	7	6	2
MAS-Com-monKADS	6	8	10	3	2
Gaia	9	4	5	6	1

Based on these aspects, the following evaluation is derived, as shown in Table 5.2 (adapted to a scale of 1 [low] to 10 [high]) without explanation of the methods.

Lind outlines that all models point to the respective view of the developers. The involved products and notations have to be used. No method gets good values above all criteria. The tool support of all methods is very poor.

5.2.7 DEVELOPMENT OF AGENT-BASED GRAPHICAL USER INTERFACES (GUIs) BY KERNCHEN

GUIs are software components that allow human–computer interaction (HCI). Adaptive characteristics for increased flexibility are essential for their effectiveness and usability, because context, tasks, environment, as well as user attributes may change.

Kernchen, Zbrog, and Dumke (2007) think that creating interfaces based on agent technology does not only follow the new paradigm of agent-based software development but leads to several striven advantages, too. Agent-based GUIs can be necessary, because of the following:

- GUIs may include complex/diverse types of interaction between components as well as to external distributed heterogeneous resources.
- Negotiation, cooperation, and competition may occur among different entities.
- Some aspects of a GUI can have autonomous characteristics.
- A modification or expansion of the system can be anticipated.

For developing agent-based GUIs, the authors propose an iterative goal-directed methodology including design patterns and creative techniques. They address the first steps of the software life cycle, mainly specification and design. Figure 5.8 visualizes the stages of their approach.

The authors outlined a tree-based approach for developing agent-based GUIs. Therefore, they presented several stages of specification and design and supposed usage of several strategies, like creative techniques and design patterns for innovative and complete architectures.

To examine the usefulness of their approach, they designed the Agent-Based e-Learning (ABEL)-GUI, an agent-based interface for the e-learning domain (Kernchen 2006).

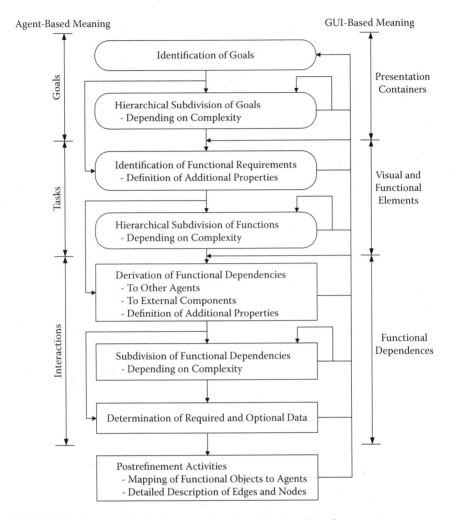

Agent-Based Meaning

GUI-Based Meaning

FIGURE 5.8   Stages of developing agent-based graphical user interfaces.

5.2.8   MAS Paradigm Evaluation by Wong, Paciorek, and Moore

MAS paradigm evaluation for mobile agent implementation with Java is presented by Wong, Paciorek, and Moore (1999). They discuss computing paradigms:

- Mobile agents reduce network traffic.
- Mobile agents provide autonomy.
- Mobile agents adapt in program state and network environment.
- Mobile agents can act asynchronously.

- Mobile agents are secure.
- Mobile agents are fault tolerant.

Using these paradigms, it is possible to evaluate different MASs using mobile agent technology.

5.2.9 MAS QUALITY MEASUREMENT BY FAR

An overview about software quality metrics for intelligent systems like software agents and MASs is given by Far (2002). Going beyond object-oriented software metrics, Far introduces a set of useful metrics for agent and MAS measurement and evaluation during the development process. He classifies the metrics into three classes for product, process, and resource measurement. An overview about the proposed metrics with basic descriptions is presented in Table 5.3.

TABLE 5.3
Software Quality Metrics for Agent and Agent System Development

Product Measurement and Evaluation	
Size estimation	This measure takes into account the functional size and the physical size of a software agent and also the agent system size.
Performance level	A set of metrics that considers the task-related performance of an agent system and the ability to realize special tasks.
Process Measurement and Evaluation	
Behavior simulation	Behavior simulation defines the degree in which the agents' behaviors within the system are implemented related to the social behavior.
Modeling of agent-based systems	This defines the model on which the construction of agent-based systems is based in respect to types of used agents and the kinds of interactions.
Agent communication language (ACL) evaluation	ACL evaluation refers to the ability of the agents in intelligent systems to communicate through common agent communication languages to better achieve collaboration and cooperation.
Reasonableness of agent deriving	The rationale behind the construction of an agent given an agent template and the possibility of deriving learning capabilities from peer agents.
Resources Measurement and Evaluation	
Middleware evaluation	Middleware evaluation is based on the communication infrastructure used to support flexibility and efficient messaging.
Vendor evaluation	Vendor evaluation considers the reliability and reputation of the vendors for agent-based components and systems.
Paradigm evaluation	The appropriateness of the chosen software basis and used software components for the implementation of software agents and the agent-based system.

5.3 MEASUREMENT EVALUATION OF MAS DEVELOPMENT RESOURCES

5.3.1 MAS Platform Evaluation by Ricordel and Demazeau

Evaluation of different MAS platforms like AgentBuilder, JACK, JADE, and Zeus is described by Ricordel and Demazeau (2000) based on evaluation criteria for complex software like MAS. Proceeding from a four-stage development process with analysis, design, development, and deployment, Ricordel defines criteria for MAS platform evaluation. The four qualities determined by Ricordel are as follows:

- *Completeness* as the degree of coverage the MAS provides for this stage. This addresses both the quantity and the quality of the provided documentation and tools.
- *Applicability* as the range of possibilities and restrictions supported by the MAS.
- *Complexity* as the required competence from the developer and the quantity of the required tasks to develop the MAS.
- *Reusability* as the quantity of work that has to be done to reuse the previous work at the MAS.

The four qualities and four stages of MAS development result in sixteen criteria for the evaluation of any MAS platform. Additionally the following other practical criteria are used:

- *Availability* as criteria, if the MAS is freely available as application and as source code.
- *Support* as criteria for future development of the MAS and if it can be used for large-scale systems.

The criteria are used to evaluate a set of MASs. Based on the criteria, Ricordel and Demazeau describe big differences between the analyzed toolkits. As a result, they explain that the difference in conceptual, methodical, and technical areas requires a standard for MAS development.

5.3.2 Measurement Study of the JADE Platform by Piccolo et al.

The measurement study of one of the most used agent platforms, JADE, is described in Piccolo, Bianchi, and Salsano (2006). The authors focus on the communication subsystem and thereby on scalability by investigating the effect of different hardware and operating systems. JADE is a Java-based middleware developed after the agent paradigm. It follows the Foundation for Intelligent Physical Agents (FIPA) standard to ensure interoperability among different intelligent MASs.

Three different operations are analyzed for the intended measurement goal. The first, the secondary container start-up measures the time between starting a container (a run-time instance of the Java Virtual Machine [JVM]) and the time when it is ready to accept user commands. It is possible to identify 16 different infinite populations of start-up times. Agent migration describes the process of transferring an agent from one container to another. The authors claim that JADE scales linearly from this point of view. Their last analysis of the interaction among agents in a changing number of containers shows that JADE's interaction performance is affected only by the number of used containers, if there are more than 300 interacting agents.

Altogether, the results show a nearly linear scalability of the JADE agent platform.

5.3.3 Performance of Open-Source Multiagent Platforms by Mulet et al.

JADE, MadKit, and AgentScape are analyzed by Mulet, Such, and Alberola (2006). The authors' goal is to determine to what extent the internal platform design influences its performance. They focus on two agent platform artifacts: for the messaging service, they are measuring the round-trip time (RTT) of each message between sender and receiver, and for the service directory service, they measure registration and deregistration times as well as the platform response time.

Results related to the messaging services include:

- One Host System
  - AgentScape performs poorest.
  - JADE and MadKit have similar responses in low load, but MadKit performs better with a higher load.
- Multiple Host System
  - AgentScape is less adaptive to size changes.
  - JADE is best in multiple message sending.
  - JADE is more scalable.

For the measuring of the service directory service, the authors present the following results:

- One Host System
  - MadKit registering service is the fastest.
  - JADE and AgentScape are slower because of a centralized service implementation
- Multiple Host System
  - AgentScape: Linear increase in search time.
  - JADE and MadKit: Constant behavior.
  - MadKit performs better than JADE.

The results show a trade-off between modularity and performance. An agent-based service implementation decreases performance. Another result shows the need for distributed services. Centralized implementations can become a bottleneck for highly demanded services.

5.3.4   EVALUATION OF JAVA-BASED AGENT TECHNOLOGIES BY KERNCHEN ET AL.

Currently, object-oriented software engineering (OOSE) is well known and well used in many industrial applications. Today, most of the problems with object orientation are understood, and some of the illusions of the "OO hype" are going in more realistic OO methods and OO techniques. In the same manner, today the future technology of agent-oriented software engineering (AOSE) can be observed.

Due to interoperability, many agent systems are implemented in Java. The evaluation of chosen representative frameworks is the focus of the work presented in Kernchen et al. (2006). They analyzed the Aglet technology of IBM research, the JADE system of the Telecom Italia Lab, and MadKit, an open source project (Table 5.4 and Table 5.5).

TABLE 5.4

Chidamber and Kemerer Metrics for Object-Oriented Software Engineering (OOSE) and Agent-Oriented Software Engineering (AOSE) Technologies

	Aglets	JADE	MadKit	Mean of AOSE	Standard Deviation of AOSE	Mean of OOSE	Standard Deviation of OOSE
DIT	0.239	0.745	0.685	0.556	0.276	0.59	0.82
NOC	0.222	0.353	0.387	0.321	0.087	0.15	0.45
WMC	10.35	9.552	8.69	9.531	0.830	8.69	7.90
CBO	5.022	6.951	5.331	5.768	1.036	3.00	4.22
RFC	25.05	15.871	21.931	20.951	4.667	14.78	16.35
LCOM	80.011	55.585	50.144	61.913	15.907	37.51	82.82

Notes: DIT = Depth of inheritance; NOC = Number of components; WMC = Weighted methods per component; CBO = Coupling between operations; RFC = Remote function call; LCOM = Lack of cohesion in methods.

TABLE 5.5

Abreu's MOOD Metrics for Object-Oriented Software Engineering (OOSE) and Agent-Oriented Software Engineering (AOSE) Technologies

	Aglets	JADE	MadKit	Mean of AOSE	Standard Deviation of AOSE	Mean of OOSE	Standard Deviation of OOSE
MHF (%)	99.87	99.84	99.75	99.82	0.062	98.77	2.92
AHF (%)	99.88	99.79	99.88	99.85	0.052	98.70	3.77
MIF (%)	17.71	40.69	59.35	39.25	20.86	25.35	22.37
AIF (%)	29.06	80.84	48.53	52.81	26.15	24.75	25.70
POF (%)	4.30	4.13	3.66	4.03	0.33	4.60	7.48

Notes: MHF = Method hiding factor; AHF = Attribute hiding factor; MIF = Method inheritance factor; AIF = Attribute inheritance factor; POF Polymorphism factor.

In general, an analysis based on metrics highlights features and supports anticipation of effects of design on external quality factors. In this chapter, three representatives of AOSE technologies using a metrics set provided by Chidamber and Kemerer and the MOOD metrics set of Abreu are analyzed. Basic results in comparison to JADE and MadKit present Aglets as less complicated, easier to maintain, but also less productive. These other two agent platforms seem to be further developed. Indications are that higher method inheritance factor (MIF) values are related to increased efficiency. MadKit contains more application-specific classes that limit the possibility of reuse and may cause maintenance problems. Outliers are mainly specialized agent classes in the *madkit.designer* package. That tends to be technology specific. Comparisons of AOSE and OOSE results prove representatives following the first paradigm are more complex. There are indications for higher testing and maintenance efforts. The higher LCOM (lack of cohesion in methods) value may lead to a focus on future research. Typically, it indicates improper use of paradigms of OO design. Being a normal attribute of AOSE is another possibility and should be further analyzed. As a summary, the following initial aspects of AOSE technology were deduced:

- AOSE is developing, as shown by increased size, complexity, and efficiency of particular frameworks over time.
- Agent technology is more complex than standard object-oriented packages. Increased testing and maintenance efforts are expected to be usual.
- AOSE representatives are making increased use of inheritance and reuse. That indicates a more efficient approach but leads to increased effort in class design.
- There are indices that OO design is not as usual for AOSE as for OOSE.

5.3.5 MEASUREMENT OF AGENT ACADEMY BY WILLE

Agent Academy is a Data Mining Framework for developing and training intelligent agents. It is an innovative research and development project that was launched in 2001 under the Information Society Technologies European Union (EU) Program. Agent Academy is based on the JAVA programming language and JADE agent architecture and should train new agents as well as retrain its own agents in a recursive fashion (Wille 2005; Figure 5.9).

In Figure 5.10, the analyzability of Agent Academy functions is presented as a measurement example. It reveals primarily values in the range of good for all analyzed agents.

Agent Academy evaluation has been presented as an example of how object-oriented metrics can be used to measure software agents. Because an agent-oriented programming language is missing, until now most agent systems were developed with object-oriented languages and techniques. Therefore, the object-oriented metrics deliver good and useful results. A large agent system like Agent Academy can be measured and evaluated with CASE tools in an effective way. The result of the evaluation was that with all agents, most of their classes and functions are in the range of the thresholds. The examples show that software measurement can detect and find critical areas.

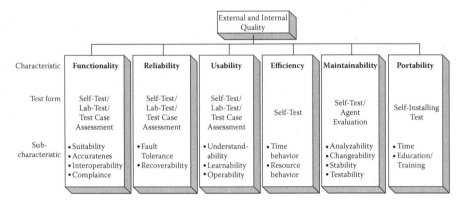

FIGURE 5.9   General quality model of Agent Academy.

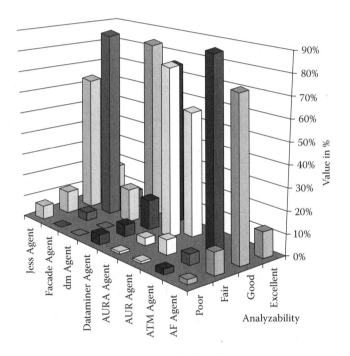

FIGURE 5.10   Analyzability of Agent Academy functions.

5.3.6 PERFORMANCE OF AGENT LOCATION MECHANISMS BY BEN-AMI AND SHEHORY

A comparative analysis of agent location mechanisms is described by Ben-Ami and Shehory (2005). Central location approaches exist like the most common central directory services and distributed approaches. These are, for example, distributed matchmaking and peer-to-peer agent location.

To examine different approaches and scenarios, the authors measured the following metrics within their MAS:

- *RefTime*, as the time to find another agent with the needed capabilities.
- *DoneTime*, as the average time for an agent's delegated task to complete.
- *HitRate*, as the ratio of successfully processed tasks and the total number of tasks.
- *MsgCount*, as the average number of incoming and outgoing messages of an agent.

Experiments on a single host system and a multiple host system were performed, and for the first series of experiments, the results are as follows:

- Single Host System
  - Response times of centralized location mechanisms are significantly higher than those of distributed mechanisms.
  - Communication overhead of distributed mechanisms does not affect scalability.
  - Response time of centralized approaches improves with decreasing workload.
  - The distributed approach is significantly better for high workloads.
  - Centralized models achieve better results for low capability distribution.
  - Distributed location models perform better with ordered connection models.
- Multiple Host System
  - Response times of the centralized location mechanism are significantly higher than for distributed mechanisms.
  - An exponential increase of message counts was experienced during a linear increase of the search horizon.

In summary, the authors suggest that distributed location mechanisms be used for large-scale MASs with high workload, but with the trade-off of the costs of a communication overhead.

5.3.7 PERFORMANCE OF MULTIAGENT LEARNING ALGORITHMS BY PANAIT AND LUKE

Panait and Luke (2006) present an analysis of evolutionary algorithms for multiagent learning. The authors focus on their idea that agents may benefit from exploring those actions that inform their teammates about the structure of the search space. Therefore, they present iCCEA, a cooperative coevolutionary algorithm.

The authors' results present their approach as delivering better results in a shorter time, but they also warn of the danger of wasting too many resources.

5.3.8 Middleware Evaluation by Poslad et al.

Selected agent platforms with respect to types of middleware services were evaluated by Poslad et al. (1999). The middleware services provided by the agent systems include message transport, directory service, agent communication, management, brokerage, and mobility. Some of these services can be broken down into subservices. The nominal evaluation of the middleware aspects in agent-based systems by Poslad et al. is presented in Table 5.6. In Table 5.6, "x" indicates that the service is available. The "–" indicates that the service is not available, and the "?" means that it is not clear.

5.3.9 Measuring Resource Usage for Self-Interested Agents by He

A task-oriented mechanism for the measurement of computational resource usage in MAS is described by He and Loerger (2005). The authors base their research on game theory to form resource-sharing coalitions among agents by automated party negotiation. They develop the metric with respect to the following principles:

- The task executed by the resource evaluates the economic value of using the resource.
- The values of two resources are equal if they can accomplish identical tasks with the same performance requirements.

TABLE 5.6
Middleware Services Offered by Some Multiagent Systems

Middleware Services	Agent Systems							
	FIPA AP	Info Sleuth	JATLite	KAoS	KIMSAC	OAA	OMG AF	ZEUS
Transport service	x	x	x	x	x	x	x	x
Forwarding	x	x	x	x	x	x	x	x
Routing	x	x	x	?	?	?	x	?
Mailbox	–	?	?	?	?	?	x	?
Directory services	x	x	x	x	?	x	x	x
White pages	x	x	?	x	?	x	x	x
Yellow pages	x	?	?	x	?	x	x	x
Management services	x	?	?	?	?	?	x	x
Message storage	x	?	?	?	?	?	x	?
Agent life cycles	?	?	?	?	?	?	x	?
Agent communication service	x	x	–	x	x	x	–	x
Organization	?	?	?	x	x	x	–	x
Coordination	x	?	?	?	?	?	?	x
Brokerage service	–	–	–	–	–	–	–	–
Mobility service	–	–	–	–	–	–	x	?

- The interactions among agents establish the economic value of resource usage.
- An established economic value changes if the relationship between the demanded and supplied amount of the resource changes also.

They define the economic value $V(k,D)$ of using a central processing unit (CPU) as a resource to finish a task k in duration D as:

$$V(k,D) = (n + \lambda_1 n_0) \times (m + \lambda_2 m_0) \times V_s \qquad (5.1)$$

Where m_0 and n_0 refer to the number of CPUs, and λ_1, λ_2 model the fact that changing the number of CPUs leads to a changed economic value.

Based on the metric, the authors propose an algorithm to form resource-sharing coalitions among agents. Experimental results show the effect of the economic-value-based decisions on the behavior of the agents.

5.3.10 Measurement of DAML+OIL Ontologies by Wille

The use of ontologies plays an increasing role in the field of MAS and is an area of active research (Maximillien and Singh 2004). For all types of communication, negotiation, coordination, and cooperation, both between agents as well as between agents and their users, ontologies are essential. Together with the development of the Semantic Web, Berners-Lee, Hendler, and Lassila (2001) explain that the effectiveness of software agents will increase exponentially as more machine-readable Web content and automated services (including other agents) become available. Agent-oriented ontology languages should allow for higher operational value in the meaning of autonomic knowledge processing. In recent years, different agent-oriented languages for the Semantic Web were developed. Therefore, the metrics shown in Table 5.7 were defined.

An initial analysis of four sample ontologies is described by Wille (2005). The validation of the measurement approach will be given as the measurement of the following four ontologies (Figure 5.11):

1. A first ontology example based on the Web presence of "Web-Systems AG," which is presented in the book "Web Engineering" (Dumke et al. 2003). This ontology includes knowledge about customer information, products, order information, and customer assessment.
2. The second example presents the measurement results of an ontology for classifying object-oriented metrics.
3. The next example presents an ontology measurement based on an ontology that supports the teaching offerings of the working group "Softwaretechnik" at the University of Magdeburg, Germany.
4. The last measured example is a classical example given by DAML (2004), and it presents an ontology for a biological organism.

TABLE 5.7

DAML (Defense Advanced Research Projects Agency Agent Markup Language) and Ontology Interface Layer (OIL) Metrics and Their Scale Properties

Shortcut	Metric	Calculation	Scale Characteristics
K	Number of classes	num_classes	Ratio scale
UK	Number of subclasses	num_subCalls	Ratio scale
P	Number of properties	num_properties	Ratio scale
UP	Number of subproperties	num_subProperties	Ratio scale
I	Number of instances	num_instances	Ratio scale
G	Size of the ontology	K+UK+P+UP+I	Ratio scale
TK	Depth in the class inheritance tree	DIT object-orientation metric	Ordinal scale
TP	Depth of the property inheritance tree	DIT object-orientation metric	Ordinal scale
K_{LEX}	Lexicographical complexity	$LK = X/Y,$ $X = \sum Elemente_{ONT}$ $Y = \sum Elemente_{GES}$	Ordinal scale
K_{LOG}	Logical complexity	$a_1+a_2+a_3+a_4$	Ordinal scale
KO	Coupling between ontologies	num_daml:imports	Potential ratio scale
VG	Connectivity	num_NMS+KO	Ratio scale
KG_{ONT}	Level of commentation	$KG_K+KG_P+KG_I$	Ordinal scale

Within the area of the presented measurement and evaluation approach for Semantic Web, all values are in the range of the experience and threshold values. For the structure metrics and the commentation level, the intervals seem to be useful in relation to the size evaluation of usable ontologies. The other metrics can be used as initial reference examples for comparison with other ontologies. This is especially true for the lexicographical complexity with its high value (0.63) of used language elements.

The following two comparisons present the DAML (Defense Advanced Research Projects Agency Agent Markup Language) and Ontology Interface Layer (OIL) measurement approach in relation to two other kinds of systems:

1. *Classical document-based Web application versus Semantic Web*: Measurements of Hypertext Markup Language (HTML)-based Web applications have shown that the link-based reference, for example, 1, has an average value of 4 (Dumke et al. 2003). For the DAML and OIL example, the value for the connectivity was 6. So, a higher complexity of the Semantic Web can be expected.

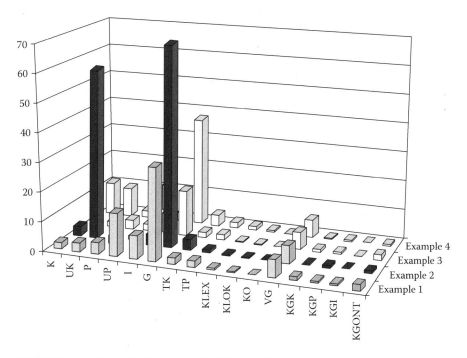

FIGURE 5.11   Metric visualization of DAML and OIL ontology measurement approach.

2. *Object-oriented software system versus Semantic Web*: Object-oriented systems typically consist of extended class libraries with hundreds of classes. The difference in values for the size metrics of DAML and OIL ontologies will be small in this point of time.

5.4   DISCUSSION

The MAS development measurement inventory shows that most measurement intentions are based on different methods of evaluating MAS. The area of MAS evaluation has no clear boundaries, and so it ranges from MAS quality evaluation to the evaluation of MAS development methods and frameworks. Metrics have been proposed for MAS measurement as well as criteria for MAS evaluation and, furthermore, a set of them is used to obtain a global quality result. An overview of the MAS evaluation approaches can be found in Figure 5.12.

This detailed view shows how many different criteria can be used to evaluate MASs during development. Unfortunately, most criteria are only named, and there is no guideline of how to measure them. The evaluation of ACLs in this sense shows how important communication aspects in MAS development are. As a result of the inventory, it can be stated that the use of measurement in MAS development is

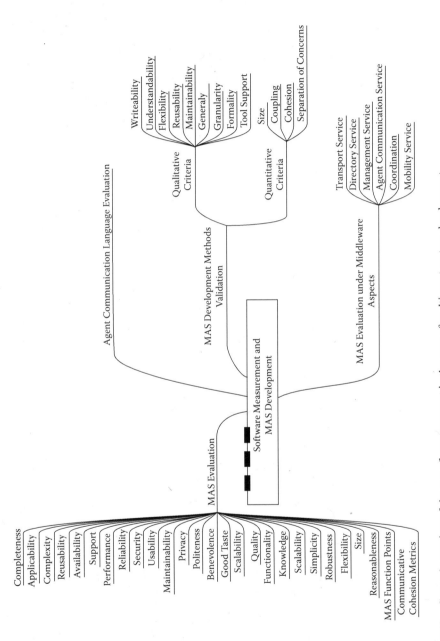

FIGURE 5.12   General overview of the use of measurement in the area of multiagent system development.

presented by only a few sources. Every source presents a set of criteria in order to evaluate MASs. Most criteria are referred to one or two times. A complex view with broad acceptance is missing.

REFERENCES

Ben-Ami, D. and O. Shehory. 2005. A Comparative Evaluation of Agent Location Mechanisms in Large Scale MAS. In *Proceedings of the 4th International Joint Conference on Autonomous Agents and Multi Agent Systems (AAMAS 2005)*, ed. F. Dignum et al., 339–346. Netherlands: Utrecht University Press.

Berners-Lee, T., J. Hendler, and O. Lassila. 2001. The Semantic Web. *Scientific American* 284(5): 34–43.

Bertolino, A., E. Marchetti, and R. Mirandola. 2002. Real-Time UML-Based Performance Engineering to Aid Manager's Decisions in Multiproject Planning. In *Proceedings of the 3rd International Workshop on Software Performance (WOSP2002)*, ed. V. Grassi and R. Mirandola, 251–261. New York: ACM Press.

DAML 2004. The DARPA Agent Markup Language Homepage. Standard Document. www. daml.org (accessed January 5, 2009).

Dimitrov, E., A. Schmietendorf, and R. Dumke. 2002. UML-Based Performance Engineering Possibilities and Techniques. *IEEE Software* 19(1): 74–83.

Dumke, R. 2003. *Software Engineering* (German). Wiesbaden, Germany: Vieweg.

Dumke, R., M. Lother, C. Wille, and F. Zbrog. 2003. *Web Engineering* (German). Munich: Pearson Studium.

Far, B. H. 2002. Performance Metrics for Intelligent Systems. Working Paper, University of Calgary. www.enel.ucalgary.ca/People/far/ (accessed January 5, 2009).

Garcia, A. F., C. J. P. Lucena, and D. D. Cowan. 2004. Agents in Object-Oriented Software Engineering. *Software-Practice and Experience* 34(5): 489–521.

He, L. and T. R. Loerger. 2005. Forming Resource-Sharing Coalitions: A Distributed Resource Allocation Mechanism for Self-Interested Agents in Computational Grids. In *The 2005 ACM Symposium on Applied Computing*, ed. J. Yen et al., 84–91. Los Altimos, CA: IEEE Computer Society Press.

Jennings, N. R. and M. J. Wooldridge. 1998. *Agent Technology — Foundation, Applications and Markets*. New York: Springer.

Juan, T. and L. Sterling. 2003. The ROADMAP Meta-Model for Intelligent Adaptive Multi-Agent Systems in Open Environments. In *Agent-Oriented Software Engineering IV, 4th International Workshop (AOSE 2003)*, ed. P. Giorgini, J. P. Müller, and J. Odell, 53–68. Berlin: Springer.

Juan, T., L. Sterling, and M. Winikoff. 2003. Assembling Agent-Oriented Software Engineering Methodologies from Features. In *Agent-Oriented Software Engineering III 3rd International Workshop (AOSE 2002)*, ed. F. Giunchiglia, J. Odell, and G. Weisz, 198–209. Berlin: Springer.

Juan, T. and L. Sterling. 2004. The ROADMAP Meta-Model for Intelligent Adaptive Multi-Agent Systems in Open Environments. In *Agent-Oriented Software Engineering IV, 4th International Workshop (AOSE 2003)*, ed. P. Giorgini, J. P. Müller, and J. Odell, 53–68. Berlin: Springer.

Kernchen, S., A. Farooq, R. Dumke, and C. Wille. 2006. Evaluation of JAVA-Based Agent Technologies. In *Applied Software Measurement*, ed. A. Abran, M. Budschuh, G. Büren, and R. R. Dumke, 175–188. Aachen: Shaker.

Kernchen, S., F. Zbrog, and R. Dumke. 2007. ABEL-GUI: An Agent-Based Graphical User Interface for E-learning. In *Proceedings of the Third International Conference on Web Information Systems and Technologies — Volume SeBeG/eL (WEBIST2007)*, 491–494. Los Altimos, CA: IEEE Computer Society Press.

Lind, J. 2001. *Iterative Software Engineering for Multiagent Systems*. Lecture Notes in Computer Science 1994, Berlin: Springer.

Lindemann, C., A. Thümmler, A. Klemm, M. Lohmann, and O. P. Waldhorst. 2002. Performance Analysis of Time-Enhanced UML Diagrams Based on Stochastic Processes. In *Proceedings of the 3rd International Workshop on Software and Performance*, ed. V. Grassi and R. Mirandola, 25–34. New York: ACM Press.

Maximillien, E. M. and M. P. Singh. 2004. A Framework and Ontology for Dynamic Web Services Selection. *IEEE Internet Computing* 8(5): 84–93.

Mulet, L., J. M. Such, and J. M. Alberola. 2006. Performance Evaluation of Open-Source Multiagent Platforms. In *Proceedings of the 5th International Joint Conference on Autonomous Agents and Multiagent Systems (AAMAS 2006)*, 1107–1109, ed. V. Grassi and R. Mirandola, 251–261. Los Altimos, CA: IEEE Computer Society Press.

Panait, L. and S. Luke. 2006. Selecting Informative Actions Improves Cooperative Multiagent Learning. In *Proceedings of the 5th International Joint Conference on Autonomous Agents and Multiagent Systems (AAMAS 2006)*, ed. P. Stone and G. Weiss, 760–766. Los Altimos, CA: IEEE Computer Society Press.

Piccolo, F., G. Bianchi, and S. Salsano. 2006. A Measurement Study of the JADE Agent Platform. In *Proceedings of the 2006 International Symposium on a World of Wireless, Mobile and Multimedia Networks (WoWMoM 2006)*, ed. M. D. Francesco et al., 638–646. Los Altimos, CA: IEEE Computer Society Press.

Poslad, S., J. Pitt, A. Mamdani, R. Hadingham, and P. Buckle. 1999. Agent-Oriented Middleware for Integrating Customer Network Services. In *Software Agents for Future Communication Systems*, ed. A. L. G. Hayzelden and J. Bigham, 221–246. New York: Springer.

Ricordel, P. and Y. Demazeau. 2000. From Analysis to Development: A Multi-Agent Platform Survey. In *Engineering Societies in the Agents World*, ed. F. Dignum and M. Graeves, 93–105. Berlin: Springer.

Singh, M. P. 1998. Agent Communication Languages: Rethinking the Principles. *IEEE Computer* 31: 40–47.

Tambe, M., D. V. Pynadath, and N. Chauvat. 2000. Building Dynamic Agent Organizations in Cyberspace. *IEEE Internet Computing* 4(2): 65–73.

Wille, C. 2005. *Agent Measurement Framework*. Ph.D., Department of Computer Science, University of Magdeburg, Germany.

Wong, D., N. Paciorek, and D. Moore. 1999. Java-Based Mobile Agents. *Communications of the ACM* 42(3): 92–105.

6 Conclusions and Future Directions

6.1 SUMMARY OF THE CURRENT SITUATION

Software agent technology is one of the key approaches to implementing self-managed and adaptive systems. In the previous chapters, a number of quality measurement methods addressing the detailed quality characteristics of the different kinds of software agents and agent-based systems were considered. Furthermore, the main quality involvements produced by using development methodologies and paradigms were also described. In this chapter, we attempt to characterize the current situations in this context. In order to evaluate these situations, different quality levels in agent-oriented software engineering (AOSE) as defined in Chapter 2 will be used. The situation of existing metrics, measurements, and case studies is characterized as (M) and (—) otherwise.

6.1.1 QUALITY MEASUREMENT OF SOFTWARE AGENTS

Different parts and components of software agents in the same manner as the classification in Chapter 2 will now be considered (see also the References in Chapter 2).

6.1.1.1 Measurement Situation of Agent Design Level

(—) *Software agent size* can be measured in the "classical" manner as lines of code, function points, and counting (see Ebert and Dumke 2007).

(—) *Software agent component structure* can be measured using "classical" component-based software engineering (CBSE) metrics (see Kandt 2006).

(—) *Software agent complexity* can be measured and evaluated using existing appropriate complexity metrics (see Zuse 1998).

(M) *Software agent functionality* can be measured as by Tewari, Maes, Develin, Scott, and Caballero.

6.1.1.2 Measurement Situation of Agent Description Level

(—) *Software agent development description level* can be determined using documentation metrics (see Kenett and Baker 1999).

(—) *Software agent application description level* should be evaluated using process measures (see Pandian 2004).

(—) *Software agent publication description level* can be measured using evidence-based metrics (see Kitchenham et al. 1997).

6.1.1.3 Measurement Situation of Agent Working Level

(M) *Software agent communication level* can be measured as communication index by Pedrycz and Vokovich.

(M) *Software agent interaction level* can be measured as coalition value by Shehory.

(M) *Software agent learning level* can be measured as intelligence factor by Hasebrook, and as communication learning by Fischer.

(M) *Software agent adaptation level* can be measured as agent service improvement by Chen.

(M) *Software agent negotiation level* can be measured by Barber, and commitment level by Chang.

(M) *Software agent collaboration level* as a service level can be measured by Bissel and Klusch.

(M) *Software agent coordination level* can be measured (as fitness) by Loia, Sessa, Eymann, Lee, and Liu.

(M) *Software agent cooperation level* can be measured as goal achievement by Norman, Long, Sycara, Russell, and Norvig.

(M) *Software agent self-reproduction level* can be evaluated by Barber and measured by Guessoum.

(M) *Software agent performance level* can be measured by execution time of Guichard and Apel, and the performance measurement and simulation by Pham, Sugawara, Tambe, Russell, Norvig, Joshi, Kotz, Kwitt, Wijata, Neruda, Gómez-Martínez, Wille, Krusina, and Evans.

(M) *Software agent specialization level* can be measured (as goal matching frequency) by Yan and Choi.

Note that this optimistic situation must be reduced by the measurement specialization of the cited measures and metrics addressed to special kinds of systems, platforms, and architectures. The inventory of agent-related measurement research approaches published in one year shows that some criteria have not yet been measured (e.g., portability, security, trustworthiness, reusability, functionality, testability, and efficiency).

6.1.2 Quality Measurement of Agent Systems

In the following, the situation of agent systems and multiagent systems (MASs) considering quality improvement and assurance are characterized.

6.1.2.1 Measurement Situation of Multiagent System (MAS) Design Level

(M) *Agent system size* can be measured using the architecture-based size measure of Evans and applying the function point count by Far.

(M) *Agent system component structure* can be determined using architecture metrics by Helsinger.

(—) *Agent system complexity* can be measured using appropriate existing complexity measures (see Zuse 1998).

(M) *Agent system functionality* can be estimated using simulation approaches like the Simple Thread Language (STL) of Schumacher.

6.1.2.2 Measurement Situation of MAS Description Level

(—) *Agent system development description level* can be evaluated using well-known process measures (see Ebert and Dumke 2007).

(—) *Agent system application description level* should be determined using existing documentation metrics (see Keyes 2003).

(—) *Agent system publication description level* can be measured considering process evaluation (see Emam 2005).

6.1.2.3 Measurement Situation of MAS Working Level

(**M**) *Agent system communication level* can be measured as (e-marketplace) communication by Pham, and as network communication by Lukschandl.

(**M**) *Agent system interaction level* can be evaluated as coordination level by Tolksdorf.

(**M**) *Agent system knowledge level* can be determined as experiences between agents by Weng.

(**M**) *Agent system lifeness level* can be determined as a kind of agent population by Liu.

(**M**) *Agent system conflict management level* can be evaluated as risk level by Collins.

(**M**) *Agent system community level* can be measured considering the social order of agents in the MAS by Egashira and Hashimoto.

(**M**) *Agent system management level* can be measured using utility, service, and device agents by Gustavsson.

(**M**) *Agent system application level* can be measured as cooperation performance by Ahn and Park, and as scalability by Rana and Stout.

(—) *Agent system stability level* can be evaluated using "classical" metrics of reliability and system stability (see Munson 2003).

(**M**) *Agent system performance level* can be measured in the business-to-business (B2B) context by Ouksel, in large distributed systems by Helsinger, and in telematics by Gerber, Gibney, Corteses, Patel, and Stojanov.

(**M**) *Agent system organization level* can be measured as coalition description by Katoh.

Note that this overview shows that some measurement approaches exist, but they do not cover all of the considered MAS characteristics.

6.1.3 QUALITY MEASUREMENT OF AGENT SYSTEMS DEVELOPMENT

In this section, the situation of the development of agent systems and MASs considering quality improvement and assurance of the processes and resources are characterized.

6.1.3.1 Measurement Situation of Agent Development Life Cycle Level

(—) *Software agent phase level* can be determined using the appropriate object orientation (OO) process metrics and experiences (see Ebert and Dumke 2007).

(—) *Software agent milestones level* can be evaluated by the well-known process measurements (see Putnam and Myers 2003).

(—) *Software agent requirements workflow level* can be characterized by the general life cycle consideration (see Pfleeger 1998).

6.1.3.2   Measurement Situation of Agent Development Method Level

(M) *Software agent methodology level* can be improved using the Unified Modeling Language (UML) extension by Bertolino and Dimitrov.

(M) *Software agent paradigm level* can be evaluated using the methodology quality aspects by Lind.

(—) *Software agent computer-aided software engineering (CASE) level* can be measured using general OO experiences and measurement approaches (see Dumke, Côté, and Andruschak 2004).

6.1.3.3   Measurement Situation of Agent Development Management Level

(—) *Agent project management level* can be evaluated using the well-known five core (process) metrics (see Putnam and Myers 2003).

(—) *Agent configuration management level* can be determined using general configuration experiences (see Juristo and Moreno 2003).

(—) *Agent quality management level* can measured using the existing process evaluation approaches like Capability Maturity Model Integration (CMMI) (see Wohlin 2000).

Now, the development process of the MAS and establish the following situation for the measurement and evaluation of these aspects will be considered.

6.1.3.4   Measurement Situation of MAS Development Life Cycle

(—) *Agent system phase level* can be determined using the appropriate OO process metrics and experiences (see Ebert and Dumke 2007).

(—) *Agent system milestones level* can be evaluated by the well-known process measurements (see Putnam and Myers 2003).

(—) *Agent system requirements workflow level* can be evaluated by the general life cycle consideration (see Pfleeger 1998).

6.1.3.5   Measurement Situation of MAS Development Method

(M) *Software MAS methodology level* can be determined using method comparison by Garcia.

(M) *Software MAS paradigm level* can be characterized using the meta-model by Juan, and the framework evaluation by Tambe, Pynadath, and Chauvat.

(M) *Software MAS CASE level* can be evaluated using the development approach ranking criteria by Lind or graphical user interface (GUI) flexibility by Kernchen.

6.1.3.6   Measurement Situation of MAS Development Management Level

(—) *System project management level* can be measured using the well-known five core (process) metrics (see Putnam and Myers 2003).

(—) *System configuration management level* can be determined using general configuration experiences (see Pfleeger 1998).

(—) *System quality management level* can measured using the existing process evaluation approaches like Software Process Improvement and Capability Determination (SPICE; see Ebert and Dumke 2007).

The agent and MAS development process require different resources, such as personnel (developer, tester, administrator, etc.), software resources (MAS commercial off-the-shelf software [COTS] and CASE tools), and platform resources, including the hardware components. Therefore, measurement values with respect to the characteristics (especially the quality) of these resources are needed. The measurement situation can be characterized as follows.

6.1.3.7   Measurement Situation of Agent Developer Level

(—) *Agent developer skill level* can be measured using the personal software process (PSP) (see Humphrey 2000).

(—) *Agent developer communication level* can be evaluated using an experience-based classification (see Jones 2007).

(—) *Agent developer productivity level* can be determined using the appropriate resource metrics (see Putnam and Myers 2003).

6.1.3.8   Measurement Situation of Agent Software Resources Level

(**M**) *Agent software paradigm level* can be measured by the evaluation approaches of Wong, Paciorek, and Moore.

(**M**) *Agent software performance level* can be measured considering the JADE platform by Piccolo or the learning algorithm of Panait and Luke.

(—) *Agent software replacement level* is based on software maintenance and migration (see Pfleeger 1998).

6.1.3.9   Measurement Situation of Agent Hardware Resources Level

(—) *Agent hardware reliability level* should be evaluated using the appropriate hardware literature (see also Pandian 2004).

(**M**) *Agent hardware performance level* can be evaluated based on the platform evaluation by Ben-Ami, Shehory, Ricordel, and Demazeau.

(—) *Agent hardware availability level* should be evaluated using the appropriate hardware literature (see also Munson 2003).

6.1.3.10   Measurement Situation of MAS Developer Level

(—) *System developer skill level* can be evaluated using the PSP (see Humphrey 2000).

(—) *System developer communication level* can be measured using an experience-based classification (see Putnam and Myers 2003).

(—) *System developer productivity level* can be evaluated using an experience-based classification (see Jones 2007).

6.1.3.11   Measurement Situation of MAS Software Resources Level

(**M**) *System software paradigm level* can be evaluated using the Agent Communication Language (ACL) evaluation criteria by Sing or adapting the paradigm comparison results by Kernchen or using the ontology evaluation by Wille.

(**M**) *System software performance level* can be measured by the middleware evaluation by Far and Poslad or the measurement of the system quality by Wille.

(**M**) *System software replacement level* can be evaluated based on the resource usage by He.

6.1.3.12   Measurement Situation of MAS Hardware Resources Level

(**M**) *System hardware reliability level* can be measured using the platform quality criteria by Ricordel and Demazeau.

(**M**) *System hardware performance level* can be measured (especially for Java-based platforms) using the approach by Mulet.

(**M**) *System hardware availability level* can be evaluated using the platform quality criteria by Ricordel and Demazeau.

As a result of the inventory of agent system (development) processes, it can be stated that the use of measurement in MAS development is presented by only a few sources. A detailed view with broad acceptance is still missing.

6.2   OPEN QUESTIONS AND FUTURE DIRECTIONS

Software agent technology is one of the key approaches to implementing global infrastructures such as self-adapting systems, self-healing applications, corporate global creation, and collaborated robotic teams. These kinds of software systems currently remain as challenges in implementing real intelligent and autonomous software systems that solve, support, or manage the worldwide society, organization, and community problems of the twenty-first century.

The role of quality and quality assurance of agent-based systems and system development is gaining importance and was described previously. The situation in agent systems quality measurement and assurance based on the software measurement discipline has been established. Therefore, the following open questions can be derived:

(**Q1**) The existing quality measurement of software agents is mainly directed to agent performance and run-time quality. Much more effort is still needed to understanding, evaluate, and *manage the new kinds of complexities in such autonomous and intelligent systems.*

(**Q2**) Agent description and documentation quality is currently based on the experiences and quality assurance technologies from the object-oriented paradigm. Here, *more analysis and case studies about the usefulness of the OO experience for MAS quality evaluation* are needed. A first step

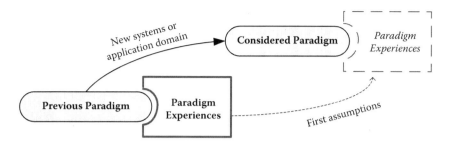

FIGURE 6.1 Software paradigms and their experiences.

could be the application of existing experiences of the other software technologies or paradigms. Therefore, the typical situation in software paradigms is that they are behind the experiences of their (first) use (see Figure 6.1).

Based on these general characteristics, the following measurement and evaluation assumptions can often be established (Dumke et al. 2007):

A simplification of the CBSE measurement and evaluation as a "further kind of object-oriented software engineering (OOSE)."

Typical situation is that service-oriented software engineering (SOSE) was understood as a "special kind of OOSE."

A simplification of the aspect-oriented programming (AOP) measurement and evaluation as a "simple extension of OOSE"

The understanding of AOSE as "OOSE with more flexibility."

These assumptions could facilitate initial measurement and evaluation in software agent development as well as application processes.

(Q3) The weaknesses in quality assurance on the agent process and resources areas must be compensated for by using the appropriate "classical" process experiences and process metrics in order to address the quality assurance of agent system development in the general, well-known manner. It is necessary *to analyze the typical and new process ingredients and key areas for software agent processes.*

(Q4) Most of the measurement approaches presented are based on direct measurement and evaluation. Quality assurance techniques for agent-based systems should include all kinds of measurement and evaluation methods, like assessment, prediction, analogies, experiments, statistical analysis, and expertise.

(Q5) The development of an MAS is based on many technologies, methodologies, and paradigms. Therefore, the *paradigm of AOSE should consider the quality technologies of all other software paradigms.* The information presented in Figure 6.2 demonstrates the complexity and costs of these technological implications. AOSE can be related to the kinds of systems (information-based, embedded, Web-based, decision support, knowledge-based, etc.) and can be based on different kinds of software development

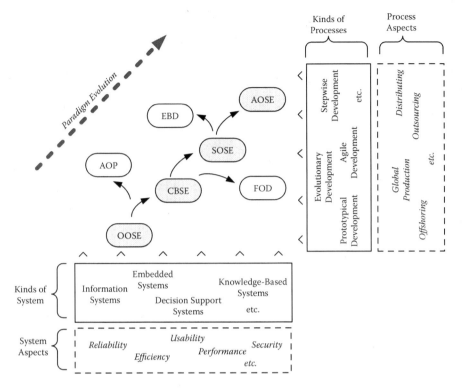

FIGURE 6.2   Software system paradigms, kinds, and aspects.

paradigms, such as OOSE, aspect-oriented programming (AOP), CBSE, feature-oriented development (FOD), SOSE, and event-based design (EBD).

On the other hand, general characteristics of software (agent) systems are meaningful in different information technology (IT) environments, such as performance, security, and usability, or context-dependent such as outsourcing and offshoring. And finally, measurement artifacts can depend upon different kinds of systems, such as embedded systems and information systems. Figure 6.2 shows the relationships between these characteristics in a simplified manner.

(Q6) Software quality assurance of agent-based systems and their development is a key problem to be faced in upcoming years. But, the *agent technologies could also be used for general quality measurement*. The general quality measurement standard ISO 15939 defines for the measurement process the following involvements (ISO/IEC 15939 2002):

> Artifacts/Objects
>> *Measured Artifacts*: The product, processes, or resources that will be measured satisfying the information needs.
>> *Collected Data*: The structure of the measures.
>> *Stored Data*: The measurement database contents.

Information Products: An indicator and its associated interpretation.
Measurement Experience Base: A data store that contains the evaluation of the information products and the measurement process as well as any lessons learned during measurement and analysis.

Measurement Tasks as Agents

Integrating Agent: For integration of the data generation and collection into the relevant processes based on the measurement of measured artifacts.

Collecting Agent: The collected data will be verified and stored, including any context information necessary to verify, understand, and evaluate the data.

Analyzing Agent: For collecting and interpreting the analyzed data according to the planning information.

Communicating Agent: For the documentation of the information products and their communication to data providers and measurement users.

Figure 6.3 shows some relationships considering the agent-based software quality measurement (Dumke et al. 2005).

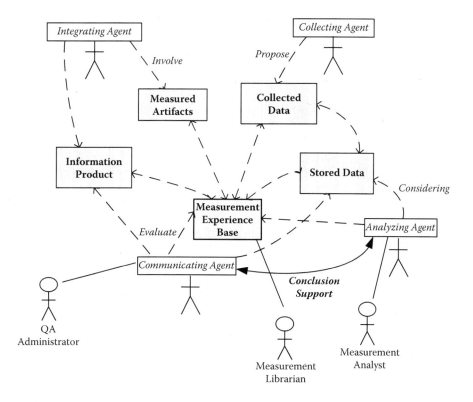

FIGURE 6.3 Performing measurement agents.

Software agent systems are more complex and difficult to manage. Their application increases every day in essential life systems following pervasive computing. Hence, the quality of the (agent-based) self-managing systems is a central point of software risks and is essential for human life and security. Therefore, it becomes necessary to analyze, evaluate, and improve the quality measurement situation.

REFERENCES

Dumke, R., R. Braungarten, S. Mencke, K. Richter, and H. Yazbek. 2007. Experience-Based Software Measurement and Evaluation Considering Paradigm Evolution. In *Praxis der Software-Messung*, ed. G. Büren, M. Bundschuh, and R. R. Dumke, 47–62. Aachen, Germany: Shaker.

Dumke, R., M. Kunz, H. Hegewald, and H. Yazbek. 2005. An Agent-Based Measurement Infrastructure. In *Innovations in Software Measurement*, ed. A. Abran and R. R. Dumke, 415–434. Aachen, Germany: Shaker.

Dumke, R., I. Côté, and O. Andruschak. 2004. Statistical Process Control (SPC) — A Metrics-Based Point of View of Software Processes Achieving the CMMI Level Four. Preprint No. 7, Department of Computer Science, University of Magdeburg, Germany.

Ebert, C. and R. Dumke. 2007. *Software Measurement — Establish, Extract, Evaluate, Execute.* Berlin: Springer.

Eman, K. E. 2005. *The ROI from Software Quality.* Boca Raton, FL: Auerbach.

Humphrey, W. S. 2000. The Personal Software Process: Status and Trends. *IEEE Software* 17: 71–75.

ISO/IEC15939 2002. *Software Engineering — Software Measurement Process.* Geneva: ISO.

Jones, C. 2007. *Estimating Software Costs — Bringing Realism to Estimating.* New York: McGraw-Hill.

Juristo, N. and A. M. Moreno. 2003. *Basics of Software Engineering Experimentation,* Boston: Kluwer Academic.

Kandt, R. K. 2006. *Software Engineering Quality Practices.* Boca Raton, FL: Auerbach.

Kenett, R. S. and E. R. Baker. 1999. *Software Process Quality — Management and Control.* Los Angeles, CA: Marcel Dekker.

Keyes, J. 2003. *Software Engineering Handbook.* Boca Raton, FL: Auerbach.

Kitchenham, B., P. Brereton, D. Budgen, S. Linkman, V. L. Almstrum, and S. L. Pfleeger. 1997. Evaluation and Assessment in Software Engineering. *Information and Software Technology* 39(11): 731–734.

Munson, J. C. 2003. *Software Engineering Measurement.* Boca Raton, FL: CRC Press.

Pandian, C. R. 2004. *Software Metrics — A Guide to Planning, Analysis and Application.* Boca Raton, FL: CRC Press.

Pfleeger, S. L. 1998. *Software Engineering — Theory and Practice.* New York: Prentice Hall.

Putnam, L. H. and W. Myers. 2003. *Five Core Metrics — The Intelligence Behind Successful Software Management.* New York: Dorset House.

Wohlin, C. 2000. *Experimentation in Software Engineering: An Introduction.* Boston: Kluwer Academic.

Zuse, H. 1998. *A Framework of Software Measurement.* Berlin: De Gruyter.

Author Index

Subject Index